GCSE

Maths

HOMEWORK BOOK

Peter Sherran
Mary Rouncefield

Letts

EDUCATIONAL

Every effort has been made to trace copyright holders and to obtain their permission for the use of copyright material. The authors and publishers will gladly receive information enabling them to rectify any error or omission in subsequent editions.

First published 1996

Letts Educational
Aldine House
Aldine Place
London W12 8AW
0181 740 2266

Text: © Peter Sherran and Mary Rouncefield 1996

Design and illustrations © BPP (Letts Educational) Ltd 1996

Design, page layout and illustrations: Ken Vail Graphic Design

British Library Cataloguing-in-Publication Data

A CIP record for this book is available from the British Library

ISBN 1 85758 414 7

Printed and bound in Great Britain by Ashford Colour Press

Letts Educational is the trading name of BPP (Letts Educational) Ltd

CONTENTS

INTRODUCTION

Welcome to your homework book. Although this book on its own is a very useful source of homework, it has been specifically written to be used with the Letts GCSE Maths classbook. You will get the most benefit if you use both books together. The numbers before the title of each of the homework sections refer to the sections of the classbook.

Like the classbook, this book has been specially written for all of the new GCSE Maths syllabuses at Intermediate level.

Each homework unit begins with a topic summary, including worked examples, to remind you of the key points when working at home. This is followed by a selection of questions, of varying styles and difficulty, arranged so that the questions become more demanding as you work through each topic. Try to follow the style of the worked examples when writing your answers so that your method is clear.

In the final section of this book, there are GCSE exam-style questions designed to help you with your revision and exam preparation, and a short checklist of things you need to know. There is also a list of important formulae at the back of the book for easy reference when answering questions.

It is becoming increasingly important to do regular homework if you want to do well. This homework book will provide a valuable way to practise and reinforce what you learn in class, and so help you to do your best and increase your enjoyment of Maths.

NUMBER SYSTEMS

The ancient Greeks and Romans used letters of the alphabet in their number systems. The Romans used the following letters.

I	V	X	L	C	D	M
1	5	10	50	100	500	1000

This system did not make use of place value and there was no symbol for zero.

For example:
LX = 60   LXX = 70   LXXXII = 82

If a letter is placed to the *left* of a letter of higher value, its value is subtracted.

For example:
IV = 4   XC = 90

By contrast, in the **decimal system** the idea of **place value** is extremely important and can be extended to include fractional values.

Whole number part				Fraction part		
... 1000s	100s	10s	1s	$\frac{1}{10}$ ths	$\frac{1}{100}$ ths	$\frac{1}{1000}$ ths ...

The position of the decimal point and the use of the zero enable us to fix the place value of each figure. The effect of multiplying, or dividing, a decimal by 10s, 100s, 1000s ... is to change the place value of all the figures, as shown by the position of the decimal point.

For example:
$230.7 = 230\frac{7}{10}$ $23.07 = 23\frac{7}{100}$ $2.307 = 2\frac{307}{1000}$ $2.307 \times 10 = 23.07$

$2.307 \times 1000 = 2307$ $2.307 \div 10 = 0.2307$ $2.307 \div 100 = 0.02307$

$6 \times 12 = 72$ $0.6 \times 1.2 = 0.72$ $0.6 \times 0.12 = 0.072$ $600 \times 0.12 = 72$

Rounding

We often need to round an answer to a level of accuracy that suits the problem. The number of figures given after the point is the number of **decimal places** (D.P.).

For example: 6.3547 may be rounded to 6.355 (3 D.P.)

6.35 (2 D.P.)

or   6.4 (1 D.P.)

The symbol < is used to stand for 'is less than' and the symbol > is used to stand for 'is more than'.

For example:
$3 < 4$ $4 > 3$ $3 < 3.5 < 4$ $6.7 < 6.72 < 6.8$ $5.3 > 5.26 > 5.2$

Questions

1.1 Ancient and Modern

1 Write the numbers from 1 to 20 using Roman numerals.

2 Write these numbers in the decimal system:
   a) LVIII   **b)** CXXI   **c)** DCCL   **d)** XD   **e)** XDII

3 The first of the modern Olympic Games was held in Athens in MDCCCXCVI. What year was this?

4 Describe any advantages that the modern decimal system has over the ancient Roman system.

1.2 Place value

5 Find the smallest numbers that can be written with these figures:
   a) 3, 8, 3, 3 and 8   **b)** 5, 4, 6, 3, and 2   **c)** 8, 1, 3, 4, 4 and 7

6 Find the largest numbers that can be written with these figures:
   a) two fours, a seven and three twos   **b)** the first five odd numbers

7 Calculate the differences between the largest and smallest numbers that can be written with these figures:
   a) 5, 1, 3, 9 and 2   **b)** 2, 4, 1, 7 and 3   **c)** 8, 7, 1, 4, and 5

8 Find the value of these and show your working clearly:
   a) $5430 - 3671$ **b)** $7500 - 4538$ **c)** $90\,000 - 15\,409$ **d)** $4000 - 1999$
   e) 5432×30 **f)** 674×400 **g)** 700×430 **h)** 800×3200
   i) 43×32 **j)** 64×45 **k)** 342×46 **l)** 712×253

9 In the binary number system, only 0s and 1s are used. The first five binary numbers are show below.
   1, 10, 11, 100, 101
   Copy and complete the pattern to show the binary numbers from 1 to 16. Find a quick way to double a number written in binary. Explain how your method works.

1.3 Extending the system

10 State the value of the 4 in each of these numbers:
   a) 74.1   **b)** 74.01   **c)** 3.42   **d)** 3.042   **e)** 340.2

11 Put these numbers in order of size, smallest first:
   a) 16.37, 16.73, 16.379, 16.399   **b)** 0.0465, 0.0564, 0.1, 0.04999

12 Write as decimals:
   a) $\dfrac{3}{10}$ **b)** $\dfrac{3}{100}$ **c)** $\dfrac{27}{100}$ **d)** $7\frac{9}{10}$ **e)** $34\frac{16}{100}$

13 Find the value of these without using a calculator:
a) 4.41×10 b) $0.73 \div 10$ c) $89 \div 10$ d) $340 \div 1000$
e) 0.043×20 f) 2.46×200 g) $46 \div 20$ h) $68 \div 2000$

1.4 Reading scales

14 What numbers do these arrows point to?

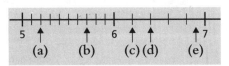

15 Show these numbers on a number line and, in each case, show the value of the mid-point:
a) 2.3 and 2.4   b) 7.48 and 7.49   c) 6.99 and 7   d) 3 and 3.1

16 Decide which of the following is nearer to 2.7183:
a) 2 or 3   b) 2.7 or 2.8   c) 2.71 or 2.72   d) 2.718 or 2.719

1.5 Decimal places

17 Round these off to a) two decimal places, b) one decimal place:
(i) 0.743   (ii) 8.497   (iii) 5.049   (iv) 0.3429   (v) 7.654218

18 Round off to the nearest penny:
a) £6.87653   b) £29.37446   c) £31 ÷ 7   d) £89.65 ÷ 11

19 Find the cost of 2137 units of electricity at 7.37p per unit.

1.6 Without a calculator

20 Copy and complete the steps below to find the value of 0.24×0.361:
     24   × 361   = 8664
     2.4   × 361   =
     0.24 × 361   =
     0.24 ×   36.1   =

     ...   .

21 Given that $38 \times 45 \times 79 = 135090$, work out the value of:
a) $3.8 \times 45 \times 79$ b) $3.8 \times 4.5 \times 7.9$ c) $380 \times 0.045 \times 79$

22 Given that $58 \times 39 = 2262$, copy and complete:
a) $? \times 39 = 22.62$ b) $580 \times ? = 226.2$ c) $? \times 0.039 = 0.2262$

1.7 More or less?

23 Compare these pairs of values and insert the appropriate symbol (< or >):
a) $0.065 \ldots 0.1$ b) $7 \ldots 0.6 \times 7$
c) $6 \ldots 6 \times 1.1$ d) $0.4 \times 0.4 \ldots 0.4 \times 0.4 \times 0.4$

24 Find any number x to make these true:
a) $8 < x < 9$ b) $6.3 < x < 6.4$ c) $0.78 > x > 0.77$ d) $0.01 > x > 0.009$

2 ANGLES AND SYMMETRY

Lines

horizontal   vertical   parallel   perpendicular

Angles

right angle 90°

acute (less than 90°)

obtuse (between 90° and 180°)

reflex (between 180° and 360°)

Angles made with intersecting lines

a b
angles on a line
$a + b = 180°$

angles at a point
$a + b + c = 360°$

vertically opposite angles
$a = c$ and $b = d$

Angles made with parallel lines

corresponding angles $a = b$

alternate angles $a = b$

interior angles
$a + b = 180°$

Angles and triangles

The sum of angles in a triangle is always 180°

hypotenuse

height

base

a right-angled triangle

120°

an obtuse-angled triangle

axis of symmetry

an isosceles triangle

60°

60°   60°

an equilateral triangle

Exterior angles of a triangle

$d = b + c$

Symmetry

Line symmetry

Rotational symmetry (order 4)

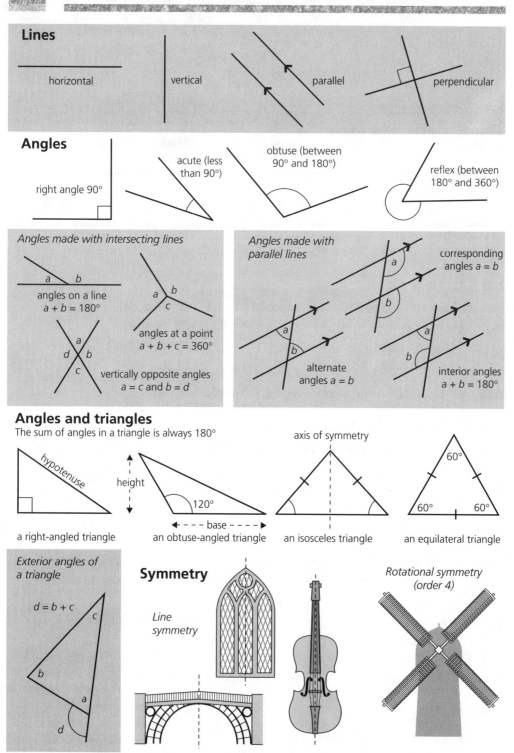

4

Questions

2.1 to 2.3 Introduction to angles and scale drawings

1 A coast guard standing on top of a cliff 100 m high observes that the angle of depression of a boat at sea is 18°. Use a scale of 1 cm to 20 m to make an accurate scale drawing. How far is the boat from the cliff?

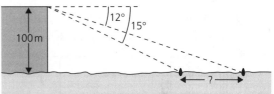

2 The coast guard also notices two buoys out at sea. The angle of depression of the first buoy is 15° and the second is 12°. If the buoys are in line with the coast guard's position, how far apart are they?

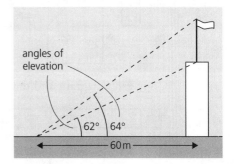

3 Anne stands 60 m away from a tower and measures the angles of elevation to a flagpole on top of the tower. The angle of elevation to the top of the flagpole is 64° and to the bottom of the pole is 62°. How tall is the flagpole? (Use a scale of 1 cm for 5 m.)

2.5 Angles and lines

4 Find the sizes of the angles marked by letters.

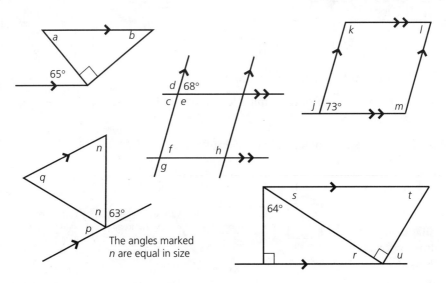

2.6 Reflections and line symmetry

5 How many axes of symmetry (lines of symmetry) does this shape have?

6 Copy each shape and draw in any lines of symmetry.

7 Copy each shape and draw in all the lines of symmetry. Write down the number of lines of symmetry underneath. (In some cases it may be zero.)

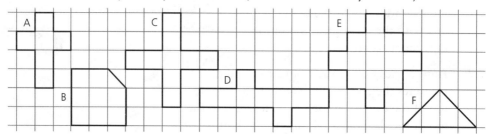

8 Copy each diagram and draw in the mirror line.

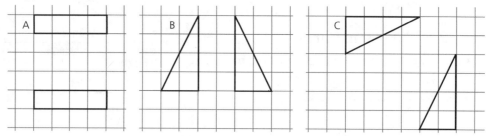

2.7 Rotational symmetry

9 Make a drawing of each of the capital letters of the alphabet which have rotational symmetry.

10 Make another set of drawings of all the capital letters which have line symmetry. Draw in all the axes of symmetry.

11 Which letters appear in both lists?

12 What is the order of rotational symmetry for each of these shapes?

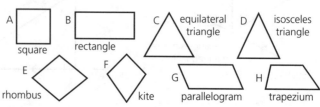

DIVISION

Division (whole numbers)
Example

Work out $2436 \div 4$.

Answer

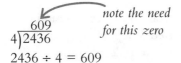

note the need for this zero

$$4\overline{)2436}$$
$$609$$
$$2436 \div 4 = 609$$

Since there is no remainder we can say that:
- 2436 is **divisible** by 4.
- 4 and 609 are **factors** of 2436.

A number is divisible by:
- 2 (i.e. it is even) if the units figure is even.
- 3 if its digit sum is divisible by 3.
- 5 if the units figure is either 5 or 0.
- 9 if its digit sum is 9.

> The **digit sum** of a number is found by adding its digits and then, if necessary, repeating the process until the result is a single figure.

A **prime** number is a whole number, greater than 1, whose only factors are itself and 1. It follows that the only *even* prime number is 2, which is also the *smallest* prime number.

Division (of decimals by whole numbers)
Example

Find $3.7 \div 4$.

Answer

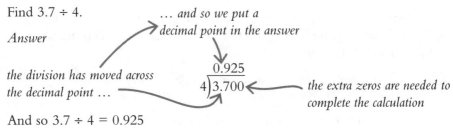

... and so we put a decimal point in the answer

the division has moved across the decimal point ...

$$4\overline{)3.700}$$
$$0.925$$

the extra zeros are needed to complete the calculation

And so $3.7 \div 4 = 0.925$

Equivalent fractions

Given any fraction, an equivalent one may be produced by multiplying (or dividing) the numerator and denominator by the same number.

Example

Which is greater out of $\frac{1}{2}$ and $\frac{3}{5}$?

Answer

$$\frac{1}{2} = \frac{5}{10} \text{ and } \frac{3}{5} = \frac{6}{10}$$

The denominator is now 10 in each case and so the fractions can be compared.

Since $\frac{6}{10} > \frac{5}{10}$, it follows that $\frac{3}{5}$ is the greater.

Percentages

1% means 1 part in 100 = $\frac{1}{100}$ = 0.01

25% means $\frac{25}{100}$ = 0.25 = $\frac{1}{4}$

17.5% means $\frac{17.5}{100}$ = 0.175

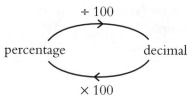

In general, an expression can be converted to a percentage by first putting it into decimal form and then multiplying by 100.

To express a mark of 47 out of 65 as a percentage, work out $\frac{47}{65} \times 100$ by keying in 47 $\boxed{\div}$ 65 $\boxed{\times}$ 100 to give 72% to the nearest whole number.

↖ *converts the fraction to a decimal*

Questions

3.1 Division of whole numbers

1 Find the value of these without using a calculator:
   a) 804 ÷ 6   **b)** 1860 ÷ 5   **c)** 918 ÷ 3   **d)** 3736 ÷ 8

2 **a)** Find the digit sum of:
   (i) 123 456 789   (ii) 234 567 891   (iii) 876 512 349   (iv) 678 912 345
   b) Write down two numbers which must both be factors of all of the above. Explain your reasoning

3 Which of the numbers below is divisible by 3? Show your method.
   a) 5436   **b)** 21 784   **c)** 576 389   **d)** 874 563

4 List the prime numbers between 100 and 130.

5 Only one of the numbers listed below is prime. Which is it? Explain your reasoning.
   a) 83 575   **b)** 83 576   **c)** 83 577   **d)** 83 579

6 **a)** Work out 7 × 11 × 13.
   b) What happens if any 3-digit number is multiplied by the answer to **a)**?
   c) Write down a 6-digit number that must be divisible by 7, 11 and 13.

3.2 Division of decimals

7 Find the value of these, making your method clear:
   a) 8.52 ÷ 6   **b)** 2.289 ÷ 7   **c)** 0.697 6 ÷ 8

8 Calculate the mean value of:
   a) 2.34, 5.12 and 4   **b)** 0.176, 0.215, 0.116 and 0.237

9   The cost of a particular model of calculator in the shops is £7.50.
A teacher purchases 30 calculators of the same type from a wholesaler for a total cost of £148.50.
a) How much does the teacher need to charge per calculator to cover the costs?
b) What is the saving for each pupil?

10   How much are the monthly payments on this TV?

3.3 Equivalent fractions

11   Copy and complete the following pairs of equivalent fractions:
    a) $\frac{5}{8} = \frac{15}{}$ **b)** $\frac{2}{3} = \frac{}{21}$ **c)** $\frac{3}{} = \frac{24}{32}$ **d)** $\frac{142}{216} = \frac{71}{}$

12   Use equivalent fractions to write these in order of size, smallest first:
    a) $\frac{3}{4}, \frac{5}{9}, \frac{2}{3}, \frac{7}{12}$ **b)** $\frac{8}{15}, \frac{3}{4}, \frac{11}{20}, \frac{5}{12}$

13   Write each of these fractions with a denominator of 10, 100 or 1000 and convert the result to a decimal:
    a) $\frac{1}{5}$ **b)** $\frac{3}{20}$ **c)** $\frac{9}{25}$ **d)** $\frac{9}{30}$

    e) $\frac{124}{200}$ **f)** $\frac{37}{200}$ **g)** $\frac{7}{125}$ **h)** $\frac{21}{70}$

3.4 Decimal patterns

14   Use a calculator to convert these fractions to decimals correct to 3 decimal places:
    a) $\frac{18}{147}$ **b)** $\frac{46}{281}$ **c)** $\frac{216}{35}$

15   Put these fractions in order of size, smallest first, by converting them to decimals:
    a) $\frac{37}{58}, \frac{29}{43}, \frac{89}{136}$ **b)** $\frac{11}{73}, \frac{18}{130}, \frac{143}{980}$

16 Write the following as recurring decimals:

a) $\frac{2}{9}$ b) $\frac{1}{22}$ c) $\frac{1}{13}$

17 a) Write $\frac{3612}{9999}$ as a recurring decimal.

b) Write $0.2\dot{7}\dot{3}$ as a fraction in its lowest terms.

18 Investigate the recurring pattern produced when the denominator of a fraction is 990. Use your findings to predict the value of the following as recurring decimals.

a) $\frac{135}{990}$ b) $\frac{247}{990}$ c) $\frac{342}{990}$ d) $\frac{1432}{990}$

3.5 Division by decimals

19 Find an expression equivalent to each of the following, such that the denominator is a whole number:

a) $\frac{1.001}{0.7}$ b) $\frac{0.037}{0.4}$ c) $\frac{0.00174}{0.03}$

20 Convert each of the expressions in question 19 to a decimal by dividing by the whole number denominator. Show your working.

21 Express $1.728 \div 9.6$ as a fraction in which the numerator and denominator are whole numbers. Cancel any common factors and complete the division.

22 Use the method of question 21 to work out $6.12 \div 1.8$.

3.6 Percentages

23 Write these percentages as decimals:
a) 43% b) 67.4% c) 9% d) 3.42%
e) 99.8% f) 0.9% g) 0.37% h) 58.25%

24 Convert these percentages to fractions in their lowest terms:
a) 25% b) 12.5% c) 37.5%

25 Write the following as percentages by first finding equivalent fractions with a denominator of 100:

a) $\frac{7}{25}$ b) $\frac{19}{20}$ c) $\frac{51}{75}$

26 Write these as percentages, correct to 2 decimal places:
a) 0.165 39 b) 0.065 31 c) 0.008 25 d) 0.934 267 1

27 Use a calculator to write these as percentages correct to 1 decimal place:
a) $\frac{47}{362}$ b) 98 out of 257 c) 973 out of 1048

PROBABILITY (1)

Probability is measured on a scale from 0 to 1. An event which is certain to happen has a probability of 1. An event which is impossible has a probability of 0.

If a game is being played using dice or cards, probabilities can be worked out by counting all the possible outcomes.

If a dice is thrown there are six possible equally likely outcomes. The probability of scoring 2 is $\frac{1}{6}$.

There are 52 cards in a pack of playing cards. The probability of picking out the two of diamonds is $\frac{1}{52}$.

The probability of picking any two is $\frac{4}{52}$ or $\frac{1}{13}$ (as there are four twos in the pack).

> **If all the outcomes are equally likely, then:**
>
> The probability of an event $= \dfrac{\text{number of ways that event can happen}}{\text{total number of different outcomes}}$

If the outcomes are *not* equally likely, then probabilities will have to be found in a different way, by investigating **relative frequencies** of events. In this case you need to collect data on a large number of events, either in an experiment or in a survey.

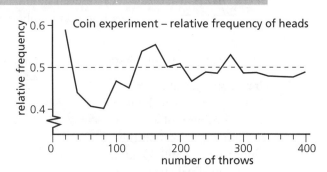

This graph shows the results of an experiment in which a fair coin was thrown 400 times. The relative frequency was re-calculated every 20 throws using:

$$\text{relative frequency} = \frac{\text{number of heads thrown so far}}{\text{total number of throws so far}}$$

You can see that the relative frequency eventually begins to level off around the value $\frac{1}{2}$.

If an experiment is repeated a large number of times the relative frequency gives us a good estimate of probability. We can use this idea to help us estimate probabilities in situations in which the outcomes are not equally likely and where we cannot work out probability in any other way.

So to estimate the probability that a person is left-handed, we calculate:

$$\text{relative frequency} = \frac{\text{number of left-handed people in our survey}}{\text{total number of people in our survey}}$$

Questions

4.1, 4.2 and 4.3 Probability, relative frequency and chance

1   A special dice with four faces is made using the
    net shown here.
    The solid shape it makes is called a tetrahedron.
    a) What is the probability that I score a 4 when
       I throw this dice?
    b) What is the probability that I score an
       even number?

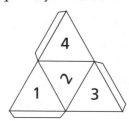

2   A game is played using this spinner.

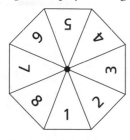

What is the probability that the
spinner will stop at:
a) number 6
b) number 7 or 8
c) a number less than 4
d) a number bigger than 4
e) an even number
f) an odd number?

3   The game in question 2 is played again using this spinner.
    Answer all the parts of question 2 again, for the new spinner.

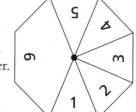

4   Draw a spinner like this.
    Divide it up so that the number 4
    has a probability of $\frac{1}{2}$.
    The other numbers on the
    spinner are 1, 2 and 3 and these
    all have an equal chance.

5   For the spinner you have drawn in question 4, what is the probability
    of scoring:
    a) number 3   b) an odd number   c) an even number.

6   There are 5 pupils in a group in a cooking class: Hannah, Mark, Vanessa, Joe
    and Sue. Two of them are to be chosen to cook a meal and serve it to some
    visitors to the school.
    You are asked to investigate the chance that Sue and her friend Joe will
    be chosen.
    a) Write down *all* the possible pairs that can be chosen from this group
       of five pupils:
       Hannah   Mark   Vanessa   Joe   Sue
       Here are three to start you off:
       H and M   H and J   H and V

b) How many different pairs did you find?

c) What is the probability that Sue and Joe are chosen? (Assume that all the pairs are equally likely to be chosen by their cooking teacher.)

d) What is the probability that Sue is one of the people chosen? (Her partner can be any of the other pupils.)

e) What is the probability that Sue is chosen with another girl?

7 I pick a card from a pack (without looking). What is the probability that it is:
a) an Ace
b) the Queen, King or Jack of spades
c) any Queen, King or Jack
d) a diamond
e) a diamond which is *not* the Queen, King or Jack
f) a red Queen
g) the Queen of spades?

8 In a game of 'Black Lady' I have the Queen of spades in my hand. I am hoping the next player will choose it from my hand. If I have six other cards in my hand, what is the probability that the next player chooses:
a) the Queen of spades
b) one of the other cards?

9 Students made a survey of the colours of cars in a car park. The table summarises their results.
Find the relative frequency of:
a) finding a black car
b) finding a car which is not red.

Colour of car	Frequency
Red	26
Black	30
Yellow	9
Green	4
Blue	15
White	11

10 A survey was carried out to determine how many people live in each house in a small housing estate. Here is the information obtained from that survey:

Number of people per house	1	2	3	4	5	6	7
Number of houses	2	8	14	10	5	1	0

Find the relative frequencies of:
a) more than four people living at a house
b) less than three people living at a house
c) one person living alone.

11 The heights of a group of
    female students were
    measured and recorded.
    The graph shows the
    results of that survey.
    Estimate the probability
    that a student selected at
    random is:
    a) less than 1.60 m tall
    b) between 1.75 m and
       1.85 m tall
    c) more than 1.70 m tall.

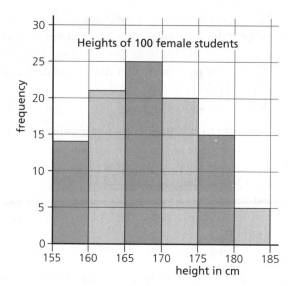

4.4 and 4.5 Random numbers and simulations

12 *Experiment*
    a) Throw a coin 400 times or find a way of simulating this experiment.
       A scientific calculator can simulate the single throw of a coin using:

       When you record your result, write down only the number before the
       decimal point, which will be either 0 or 1.
       Take 0 as tails and 1 as heads.
    b) Count the number of heads you obtain every 20 throws.
    c) Calculate the relative frequency every 20 throws.
    d) Plot a graph showing the relative frequency every 20 throws.
    e) If you used a real coin for this experiment, use your graph to decide
       whether you think your coin is a 'fair' coin.

WORKING WITH FRACTIONS

Fractions

Example

During a yacht race, four members of the crew take turns to cover an 11 hour watch during one of the stages. How long is each share of the duty?

Answer

The number of hours is given by $11 \div 4$ which can be written as $\frac{11}{4}$.

This kind of fraction, in which the numerator is greater than the denominator, is known as a **top-heavy**, or **improper**, fraction.

$\frac{11}{4} = 2\frac{3}{4}$

4 fits into 11 twice

... with 3 left over

$2\frac{3}{4}$ is called a **mixed number** because it is made up of a mixture of a whole number and a fraction.

Each share of the duty lasts $2\frac{3}{4}$ hours.

To find a fraction of an amount, the fraction and the amount are multiplied together.

Example

How long is $\frac{4}{5}$ hour, in minutes?

Answer

$\frac{4}{5}$ of $60 = \frac{4}{5} \times 60 = \frac{48}{1} = 48$. It follows that $\frac{4}{5}$ hour is 48 minutes.

Example

Work out 0.271 43 of a day in hours and minutes.

Answer

Using a calculator, $0.271\,43 \times 24 = 6.514\,32$

To convert the decimal part of an hour into minutes, subtract 6 so that the display changes to 0.514 32 and then calculate this part of 60 minutes. Check that this works out as 6 hours 31 minutes (to the nearest minute).

Significant figures

Rounding is carried out in the same way as for decimal places but this time to the figures with the highest place value.

Example

What is 3821 to 1 S.F. ... 2 S.F.?   What is 36.98 to 1 S.F. ... 2 S.F. ... 3 S.F.?

Answer

3821 = 4000 to 1 S.F   36.98 = 40   to 1 S.F.
3821 = 3800 to 2 S.F.   36.98 = 37   to 2 S.F
                              36.98 = 37.0 to 3 S.F.

5 Working with fractions

One way to estimate the result of a calculation is to round each of the numbers to 1 S.F. and then evaluate the simpler expression.

Example

Estimate the value of 9.8763×0.00615478.

Answer

Rounding to 1 S.F.: $9.8763 \times 0.00615478 \approx 10 \times 0.006 = 0.06$

This compares with a calculator answer of $\boxed{0.0607864537}$

Percentages

$50\% = \dfrac{1}{2}$ $\qquad 25\% = \dfrac{1}{4}$ $\qquad 12\frac{1}{2}\% = \dfrac{1}{8}$ $\qquad 33\frac{1}{3}\% = \dfrac{1}{3}$ $\qquad 10\% = \dfrac{1}{10}$

25% of $32 = \dfrac{1}{4}$ of $32 = 8$

$66\frac{2}{3}\%$ of $21 = \dfrac{2}{3}$ of $21 = 2 \times 7 = 14$.

Using a calculator, 17.5% of £$47.98 = 0.175 \times$ £47.98
$$= \text{£}8.40 \text{ to the nearest penny.}$$

Questions

5.1 Fractional parts

1 Convert these improper fractions to mixed numbers:

a) $\dfrac{11}{2}$ b) $\dfrac{16}{3}$ c) $\dfrac{14}{5}$ d) $\dfrac{27}{8}$ e) $\dfrac{37}{4}$ f) $\dfrac{23}{6}$ g) $\dfrac{119}{2}$ h) $\dfrac{238}{5}$

2 Work out as mixed numbers:

a) $19 \div 2$ b) $37 \div 4$ c) $28 \div 3$ d) $52 \div 5$
e) $33 \div 4$ f) $39 \div 10$ g) $25 \div 8$ h) $143 \div 20$

3 In these questions, cancel the improper fraction before converting to a mixed number:

a) $150 \div 40$ b) $77 \div 14$ c) $96 \div 36$ d) $80 \div 25$
e) $108 \div 16$ f) $950 \div 350$ g) $8000 \div 4500$ h) $168 \div 48$

4 Find the number of minutes in these fractions of an hour:

a) $\dfrac{7}{12}$ b) $\dfrac{11}{20}$ c) $\dfrac{4}{15}$ d) $\dfrac{3}{4}$

5 Use a calculator to work out these parts of a day in hours and minutes to the nearest minute:

a) 0.8765 b) 0.2796 c) 0.5618 d) $\dfrac{5}{11}$ e) $\dfrac{8.93}{47}$ f) $\dfrac{2.138}{16.74}$

6 If you sleep, on average, for 8 hours a day, what fraction of a day is this? If you live for 75 years, how much time will you spend sleeping?

7 Lisa and Helen work at a bank on a job-share scheme. Each week, Lisa works 3 days and Helen works 2 days.
a) What fraction of a week does each of them work?
b) If the total annual salary for the post is £9720, how much should each receive?

8 James is driving at a steady speed on the motorway and has travelled 48 miles in the last 55 minutes. The next services are signposted at 17 miles and 43 miles.
a) Write the distance to the first services as a fraction of the distance travelled so far on the motorway. How long should it take to reach the first services?
b) How much longer would it take to drive on to the second services?

9 An athlete's time for running the 1000 m is 2 minutes 8 seconds. Calculate the corresponding time over 800 m to the nearest second.

5.2 Significant figures

10 Round to 1 significant figure:
a) 68 432   b) 0.002 379   c) 2.099 9

11 Round to 3 significant figures:
a) 765 990   b) 1 874.68   c) 3.547 2
d) 2.497   e) 0.003 420 9   f) 89 990

12 Calculate to 2 significant figures:
a) 4200×1.76 b) $0.436 \div 237$ c) $0.0136 \times 0.002\,78$

13 The distance of the Earth from the Sun is approximately 150 million km and light from the Sun takes approximately 8.3 minutes to reach the Earth.
a) If light from the Sun takes approximately 5.8 minutes to reach Venus, find to 2 S.F. the distance of Venus from the Sun.
b) How long should it take light to reach Pluto from the Sun given that the distance between them is approximately 5923 million km? Give your answer to 2 S.F.

5.3 Estimation

14 Estimate the values of these calculations by rounding the numbers to 1 S.F.:
a) 29.8743×403.6972 b) 623.21×2.9734 c) $6437 + 5921$
d) $0.073\,468 + 0.009\,7234$ e) $78\,743 - 41\,286$ f) $610.87 \div 27.846$

15 State whether each of the approximations given below is an under-estimate or an over-estimate. Explain your reasoning.
a) $57.2654 \times 3.8976 \approx 60 \times 4 = 240$
b) $0.038\,749 \times 0.196\,345 \approx 0.04 \times 0.2 = 0.008$
c) $7.142\,36 \times 23.098\,19 \approx 7 \times 20 = 140$
d) $11.986\,75 \div 3.297\,84 \approx 12 \div 3 = 4$
e) $31.3747 \div 4.826\,73 \approx 30 \div 5 = 6$

16 Consider the calculation $84\,960 + 3641 + 16$.
If each number is rounded to 1 significant figure, does this provide a
sensible estimate?
What are the problems?
What about subtraction?
Investigate further and describe your findings carefully.

5.4 Percentages of an amount

17 Work out:
a) 50% of 38 b) 20% of 45 c) 25% of 44
d) $33\frac{1}{3}$% of 96 e) $12\frac{1}{2}$% of 48 f) $66\frac{2}{3}$% of 36

18 Find 10% of each of the following amounts:
a) £50 b) £700 c) £360 d) £47.60 e) £74.30
f) £212.80 g) £65 h) £347 i) £6

19 Estimate the value of these by rounding the amounts to the nearest £ first:
a) 25% of £47.87 b) 20% of £35.17 c) $33\frac{1}{3}$% of £51.31
d) $12\frac{1}{2}$% of £19.85 e) 25% of £14.83 f) 20% of £7.97

20 Find: a) 10% of £86 b) 5% of £86 c) 2.5% of £86

21 Show how your answers to question 20 can be used to calculate 17.5% of £86.

22 Calculate the 'now' prices for these labels.

was **£96** now

was **£243** now

was **£72.99** now

SALE 33⅓% OFF!

23 Calculate to the nearest penny:
a) 17.5% of £36.99 b) 12.5% of £186.45 c) 9.3% of £235.64

24 Find to 3 significant figures:
a) 0.27% of 8.63 m b) 89.9% of 549 kg c) 27.81% of 864 tonnes

25 Make efficient use of a calculator to find the VAT at 17.5% on these amounts:
a) £47 b) £136 c) £2687 d) £11.98
e) £6.89 f) £9865 g) £23789 h) £612.47

ORGANISING DATA

There are three different ways of expressing typical or average values.

Example

Nick has asked his friends how many videos or films they watched in the last week. Their answers were:

10 6 1 0 2 3 7

Find the mean and median of this set of results.

Answer

The mean is given by:

$$\text{mean} = \frac{10 + 6 + 1 + 0 + 2 + 3 + 7}{7} = \frac{29}{7} = 4.14$$

> The **mean** is found by adding the results and dividing that total by the number of results used.

To find the median, the results must be arranged in order:

0 1 2 3 6 7 10

> The **median** is the middle value in a set of results.

The middle value is 3, so the median is 3 videos.

Example

Another of Nick's friends watched 10 videos. Find the median and mode of this new set of results:

0 1 2 3 6 7 10 10

Answer

If there is an even number of results, the median is halfway between the two middle results.

The median is halfway between 3 and 6.

$$\text{median} = \frac{3 + 6}{2} = \frac{9}{2} = 4.5$$

The mode of these results is 10.

If a number of results are organised into a frequency table, the mode is the result with the highest frequency.

> The **mode** is the result which occurs with the greatest frequency (i.e., most often).

Range

The range gives you an idea of how spread out the results are.

The range of 0, 1, 2, 3, 6, 7, 10 and 10 (from the example above) is found by:

range = largest result − smallest result = 10 − 0 = 10.

> The **range** of a set of values is the difference between the highest value and the lowest value.

Pie charts are useful for illustrating categorical data. They show the proportion of the total for each category.

How to draw a pie chart
1 Find the total for the categories or items listed
2 Find the fraction of the total for each item
3 Multiply this fraction by 360° to find the angle for each item

Joe used this table to work out his pie chart.

Activity	Time (hours)	Fraction	Angle
Sleeping	8	$\frac{8}{24}$	120°
At school	$6\frac{1}{2}$	$\frac{6\frac{1}{2}}{24}$	98°
Eating	1	$\frac{1}{24}$	15°
Watching TV	3	$\frac{3}{24}$	45°
Athletics	2	$\frac{2}{24}$	30°
Listening to radio	$1\frac{1}{2}$	$\frac{1\frac{1}{2}}{24}$	23°
Homework	2	$\frac{2}{24}$	30°

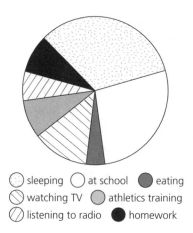

sleeping   at school   eating
watching TV   athletics training
listening to radio   homework

Questions

6.1 Which kind of average?

1 The numbers 3, 5, 8, 10 and x have a mean equal to 8. Find the value of x.

2 What additional number must be included in the following list to make the median of the six numbers equal to 4?
     1, 10, 5, 15, 2

3 Six people get into a lift. If their mean weight is 68.4 kg, what must their total weight be?

4   The librarian conducted a survey of the number of pupils going to the school library at morning break for two weeks, one in summer, one in winter.

Find the mean, median, mode and range for each week. Which week was the summer week, week 1 or week 2? Explain your answer.

Week 1	26	19	28	24	21
Week 2	12	7	8	9	20

6.2 to 6.3 Ways of displaying data

5   The bar chart shows which items children spend their pocket money on.
   a) Roughly what percentage of children say they spend their pocket money on crisps, sweets and ice cream?
   b) Which item do fewest children buy?
   c) What percentage of children buy books and stationery?
   d) Can you tell *how much* money children spend on each item?
   e) Do the percentages add up to 100?
   f) What question(s) were the children asked?
   g) What do you think was the purpose of the survey?
   h) Are you convinced by it?

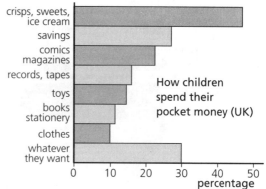

How children spend their pocket money (UK)

6   Roughly 60% of the total broadcasting time by BBC network radio is devoted to music of all kinds. Here are the percentages of total time devoted to some other categories in 1970 and 1990.
   a) Draw a bar chart to show these results, showing 1970 and 1990 side-by-side for each category as shown below.

Category of programme	Percentage of total 1970	1990
Documentaries	15.5	22.6
News	6.9	6.7
Sport	2.2	5.3
Drama	4.8	2.9
Light entertainment	2.2	2.0

b) Which categories have hardly changed?
c) Which categories have increased?
d) Which categories have decreased?

7 The results of an opinion poll are to be shown on a pie chart. The angle corresponding to 'don't know' is 18°. If there were 1500 people in the survey, how many of them gave the answer 'don't know'?

8 The pie chart shows the sales of various flavours of crisps at the school shop in one week.
a) What percentage of sales did cheese and onion have?
b) If beef accounted for $12\frac{1}{2}$% of total sales, calculate the angles x and y.

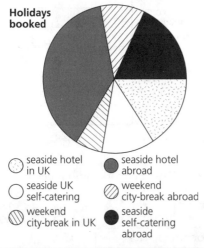

cheese and onion

plain
$y°$

81°

120°

$x°$

salt and vinegar

beef

9 This pie chart shows the numbers of people booking different kinds of holidays at a travel agency, in one week.

Holidays booked

seaside hotel in UK
seaside hotel abroad
seaside UK self-catering
weekend city-break abroad
weekend city-break in UK
seaside self-catering abroad

a) Which kind of holiday was most popular?
b) Which kind of holiday was least popular?
c) Were all UK holidays taken as a group together more popular or less popular than all foreign holidays?
d) If 19 people booked seaside hotel holidays abroad, how many people (roughly) were there who booked self-catering holidays abroad?
e) Work out the angles for this pie chart – then check that they have been drawn correctly:

Type of holiday	Number of people	Fraction	Degrees in pie chart
Seaside hotel UK	8	$\frac{8}{50}$	$\frac{8}{50} \times 360° = 58°$
Self-catering UK	6	$\frac{6}{50}$	
City-break UK	3		
Seaside hotel abroad	19		
City-break abroad	5		
Self-catering abroad	9		
	TOTAL =		TOTAL =

f) What is the total for the degrees in a pie chart? (You can always use this to check that you are right.)

10 Decide on which activities you would include in a pie chart showing a day in your life. (Do not include too many small categories.) Draw your pie chart.

PROCESS AND PRIORITY

Checking

Two commonly used methods for checking answers to calculations are:
a) estimation   **b)** reversing the process.

Both methods avoid the problem of simply repeating the original error in the checking process.

The calculation $5.86 \times 6.25 = 26.625$ is clearly wrong since an under-estimate of the answer is given by $5 \times 6 = 30$

On the other hand, the calculation $\frac{1}{3}$ of $59.94 = 19.89$ appears to be about the right size; but reversing the process gives $19.89 \times 3 = 59.67$ which again shows that there must be an error.

Equations and expressions

A statement containing an '=' sign such as $x + y = 180$ is called an **equation**. Expressing information in the form of an equation is frequently an important step in the problem-solving process.

Expressions in algebra can often be simplified. Some examples are:
$x + x = 2x$

$2y + 3y = 5y$

$2xy + 3xy = 5xy$

$5x + 3y - 2x + y = 3x + 4y$

$x \times x = x^2$

$x \times x^2 = x^3$

$2x \times 3y = 6xy$

$5xy \times 3x = 15x^2y$

Note, however, that expressions such as $3x + 4y$ cannot be simplified

When finding the value of an expression, the order in which the steps are carried out is very important. In general, the operations should be performed in the following order:

$$\boxed{\text{Brackets}} \longrightarrow \boxed{\text{Powers and roots}} \longrightarrow \boxed{\begin{array}{c}\text{Multiplication}\\\text{and division}\end{array}} \longrightarrow \boxed{\begin{array}{c}\text{Addition and}\\\text{subtraction}\end{array}}$$

Using a number line

Inequalities can be represented on a number line.

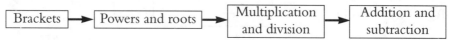

$$-2 < x \le 3$$

The operations of addition and subtraction can also be shown on a number line.

this negative sign switches the direction

From the diagram $-4 - 3 = -7$ and $-2 - -5 = -2 + 5 = 3$

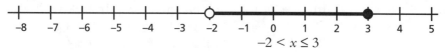

◄──── **subtract**   **add** ────►

Questions

7.1 Checking calculations

1   Use estimation to check which of the following statements must be false. Explain your reasoning for each false statement.
   a) $7.438 \times 6.185 = 41.00403$ b) $7.438 \times 6.185 = 46.00403$
   c) $34.2 \times 0.95 = 32.49$ d) $34.2 \times 0.95 = 35.49$
   e) $6.785 + 18.976 = 27.561$ f) $6.785 + 18.976 = 25.761$

2   Describe the process that would undo each of the following:
   a) add 9.87   b) divide by 6.71
   c) subtract 11.823   d) multiply by 0.764.

3   Work these out without using a calculator and check your answers by reversing the process. Show all the necessary working.
   a) $87261 - 46539$ b) $4000 - 5643$ c) $5427 \div 3$ d) $36.4 \div 0.2$

7.2 Making statements

4   Write the following statements as equations:
   a) The value of y may be found by doubling the value of x.
   b) The value of p is 4 more than the value of q.
   c) Subtracting 8.1 from the value of m gives the value of n.
   d) The product of x and y is equal to the sum of p and q.

5   Make each of the following the subject of an equation:
   a) p b) u c) s
   d) q e) r f) t

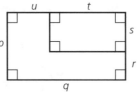

7.3 Simplifying expressions

6   Simplify these expressions, where possible:
   a) $x + x + x$ b) $4n + 2n + n$ c) $6t - 5t$ d) $4x + 3y$
   e) $x \times x \times x \times x$ f) $4x \times 3y$ g) $2xy + 3xy$ h) $5az + 2za$
   i) $4x + 2y - x - y$ j) $6ab \times 3a$ k) $ab^2 + ab^2$ l) $a^2b + ab^2$
   m) $6pq \times 5qr$ n) $6pq - 5qr$ o) $6x + 3y + xy - 2x + y + 4yx$

7   A rectangle has length l, width w and perimeter P. Write an equation giving P in terms of l and w.

7.4 Order of operations

8   Draw a flow diagram for each of these equations:
   a) $y = 5x^2$ b) $y = (x + 5)^2$ c) $y = x^2 + 5$ d) $y = 3\sqrt{x} - 6$

   e) $y = 2\sqrt{x} - 7$ f) $y = \dfrac{x + 6}{5}$ g) $y = \dfrac{x}{5} + 6$ h) $y = \dfrac{x^2 + 3}{5} - 1$

9 Given that $n = 5$, find the value of:

a) $2n^2$ b) n^3 c) $\sqrt{n+4}$ d) $(3n - 11)^2$ e) $4 + \dfrac{n+1}{2}$

7.5 Using a calculator

10 Find the value of these. In each case the answer should be a whole number.

a) $\dfrac{5.83 + 15.83}{3.8} - 2.7$ b) $\dfrac{175.01}{27.38 - 17.92} + 1.5$ c) $\sqrt{256.19 + 67.81}$

11 Given that $x = 4.87$ and $y = 3.14$ find, to 3 significant figures, the value of:

a) x^2y b) xy^2 c) $\dfrac{x+y}{x-y}$ d) $\sqrt{x} + y$ e) $\sqrt{\dfrac{x}{y}}$

7.6 Using a number line

12 List these numbers in order of size, smallest first:

a) $6.7, -8.2, -9, 4.62, -0.96$ b) $-19.8, -11.7, -23.5, 0, -6.4, 1, -18.3$

13 Draw number lines to show each of these inequalities:

a) $x > -3$ b) $x \leq -1$ c) $-2 \leq x < 3$ d) $-4 < x \leq -2$

14 Which of the following values of x satisfy the inequality $-7.5 < x \leq -5.5$?

a) -6 b) -7 c) -7.5 d) -5 e) -5.5 f) -5.4 g) -5.6

15 Copy and complete:

a) $? - 3 = -2$ b) $? + 4 = -1$ c) $? + 5 = -1$ d) $? - 7 = -9$
e) $-2 + ? = 4$ f) $-3 - ? = -7$ g) $-6 + ? = 0$ h) $-3 + ? = -3$
i) $5 + ? = 3$ j) $-3 - ? = 0$ k) $-5 - ? = 9$ l) $-2 - (-3 + ?) = -10$

7.7 Negatives in real solutions

16 These figures show the kind of information that might be included on a bank statement.

a) Why do some figures have an asterisk attached to them?

b) Copy and complete the details of these calculations taken from the statement.

(i) $? + 31.46 =$

(ii) $? - 50 =$

Debits	Credits	Balance
		147.88★
	31.46	116.42★
50		166.42★
	876.52	710.10

c) Express the details of the third transaction in the same way.

17 The first of the Ancient Olympic Games was held at Olympia in 776 BC. Boxing was included for the first time 88 years later.

Copy and complete the details of the following calculation to find the year in which boxing was introduced.

   $\ldots + 88 = \ldots$

LENGTH, WEIGHT & CAPACITY

Measuring length

Metric length

10 millimetres (mm)	= 1 centimetre (cm)
100 centimetres	= 1 metre (m)
1000 millimetres	= 1 metre
1000 metres	= 1 kilometre (km)

Imperial length

12 inches (in)	= 1 foot (ft)
3 feet	= 1 yard (yd)
1760 yards	= 1 mile

Approximate conversions

1 inch is about $2\frac{1}{2}$ cm

1 foot is about 30 cm

1 yard is about 90 cm

$\frac{5}{8}$ mile is about 1 km

Measuring weight

Metric weight

1000 mg	= 1 gram (g)
1000 g	= 1 kg
1000 kg	= 1 tonne

Imperial weight

16 ounces (oz)	= 1 pound (lb)
14 lb	= 1 stone
8 stones	= 1 hundredweight (cwt)
20 cwt	= 1 ton

Approximate conversions

1 kg is about 2.2 lb

125 g is about 4 oz

Measuring capacity

Metric capacity

1000 ml	= 1 litre
100 cl	= 1 litre

Imperial capacity

20 fluid ounces	= 1 pint
2 pints	= 1 quart
8 pints	= 1 gallon

Approximate conversions

1 litre is about $1\frac{3}{4}$ pints

300 ml is about 1 fluid ounce

1 gallon is about $4\frac{1}{2}$ litres

Questions

8.1 Measuring length

1   How many millimetres are there in:

    a) 8 cm   **b)** 9.2 cm   **c)** 6.3 cm   **d)** 59.1 cm

    e) 530 cm   **f)** 6 m   **g)** 9.4 m   **h)** 2 km?

2   How many centimetres are there in:

    a) 83 mm   **b)** 104 mm   **c)** 5 mm   **d)** 695 mm

    e) 6 mm   **f)** 6 m   **g)** 8.9 m   **h)** 2 km?

3 How many metres are there in:

a) 148 cm   b) 30 cm   c) 565 cm   d) 2 km   e) 2.8 km   f) 5000 mm?

4 A kitchen wall is 3.35 m long. Along that wall we wish to fit the following kitchen units:

    small cupboard   500 mm across
    single drawer unit   500 mm across
    washing machine   600 mm across

a) How much space will these units need?
b) Will we have room to fit the refrigerator on the same wall if it also measures 600 mm?

5 Is 1 metre more or less than 1 yard?

6 A plank of wood 10 feet long is cut into six equal lengths to make some shelves. How long is each shelf in inches?

7 Mr Johnson is 6 feet tall. Can he walk through a doorway 2 m high (without bending down)?

8 I can buy 1 m of curtain fabric for £5.50 or 1 yard for £5. Which is the best value? Should I measure my curtains in yards or metres?

9 Mount Everest is estimated to be 5.5 miles above sea level. How many feet is this correct to the nearest thousand?

10 Measure the size of the pages in this book, giving the height and width as accurately as you can in inches.

8.2 Measuring weight

11 How many kilograms are there in 7200 grams?

12 A cat eats 1 tin of cat food every day. Each tin contains 390 g of food. How much does the cat eat in one week? Give your answer in kilograms.

13 A bag of flour weighs 1.5 kg. A recipe for a chocolate cake use 175 g of flour. How many cakes can be made from one bag of flour?

14 a) In their school Ecology Week year 10 pupils collected aluminium foil, milk bottle tops and foil food containers for re-cycling. The amounts collected by three classes were: 2.56 kg, 1.82 kg, 983 g
    What was the total weight they collected?
b) If this weight is converted into pounds, is it closest to:
    (i) 5 lb   (ii) 0.5 lb   (iii) 12 lb   (iv) 120 lb?

15 a) Mr Smith weighs 12 stones. Convert this to pounds.
b) Is Mr Smith's weight in kg closest to:
    (i) 75 kg   (ii) 7.5 kg   (iii) 750 kg   (iv) 330 kg?

16 If I use 875 g of sugar and take it from a bag containing 1.6 kg, how much sugar is left in the bag?

17 a) A mother has twin babies weighing 3.2 kg and 2.88 kg. What is their combined weight in kg?

b) In lb, the total for the twins' weight is approximately:
(i) 3 lb   (ii) 13 lb   (iii) 6 lb   (iv) 130 lb?

c) How much did you weigh when you were born, in kg, ... in lb?

8.3 Measuring capacity

18 Change 2.7 litres to millilitres.

19 How many 5 ml spoonfuls are there in 1 centilitre?

20 Find the total, in litres, of 275 ml, 550 ml and 620 ml.

21 A carton of orange juice contains 0.75 litres. How many 250 ml glasses can be filled from this carton?

22 One litre is approximately equal to a pint and three quarters.
How many ml are there in 1 pint? Is it:
a) 500   **b)** 570   **c)** 1750   **d)** 430?

23 Will the contents of a 330 ml can of cola fit into a half pint glass?
Explain your answer.

8.4 Conversion graphs

24 Last time I travelled to the USA I received $1.48 for every pound sterling I changed at the bank.
a) How many US dollars did I get for £5?
b) How many dollars for £10?
c) How many dollars for £100?

25 **a)** Use your answers to question 24 to plot a conversion graph to convert amounts up to £100 into US dollars (show £ on the horizontal axis and dollars on the vertical axis).
Use your graph to answer parts **b)** and **c)**.
b) How many dollars did I get for £43?
c) My friend returned home with $35. How many pounds sterling was this worth?

SIGNS, EQUATIONS, SEQUENCES

Directed numbers

The effect of multiplying or dividing by a negative number can be shown on a diagram in which a change of direction is indicated.

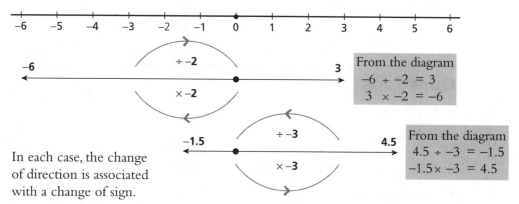

In each case, the change of direction is associated with a change of sign.

Equations

Example

Solve $3x - 7 = 4$.

Answer

We want to find a value of x so that both sides of the equation have the same value. One method is to make a flow diagram based on the equation:

$$x \rightarrow \boxed{\times 3} \rightarrow \boxed{-7} \rightarrow 4$$

The equation may now be solved by reversing the process:

$$x \leftarrow \boxed{\div 3} \leftarrow \boxed{+7} \leftarrow 4$$

The solution given by the flow diagram is:

$$x = \frac{11}{3} = 3\tfrac{2}{3}$$

Sequences

A list of numbers in a particular order, that follows some rule for producing further values, is called a **sequence**. Each value in the list is referred to as a **term**. A useful way to describe a sequence is to give a rule that relates the value of each term to its position.

Example

If we use the letter n to stand for the position of a term, what is the nth term in the sequence 2, 4, 6, 8, 10, ... ?

Answer

Each term in the sequence 2, 4, 6, 8, 10, ... is 2 × its position number. So the nth term is given by $2n$, which we may state by writing $u_n = 2n$.

The **triangle numbers** form a sequence in which the differences between the terms increase by 1 each time. The first 10 triangle numbers are 1, 3, 6, 10, 15, 21, 28, 36, 45, 55. The triangle numbers may be described by

$u_n = \dfrac{n}{2}(n+1)$.

$u_1 = 1$ $u_2 = 3$ $u_3 = 6$ $u_4 = 10$

Questions

9.1 Changing signs

1 Find the value of:

a) -5×-6 b) 2×-9 c) -9×2

d) 3×-1.2 e) -10×0.4 f) $(-3 \times -5) \times -1$

2 Copy and complete:

a) $-3 \times \ldots = -12$ b) $-7 \times \ldots = 35$ c) $\ldots \times -11 = 22$

d) $\ldots \times 6 = -48$ e) $\ldots \times -10 = 47$ f) $\ldots \times -98.73 = 0$

3 Work out:

a) $36 \div -9$ b) $-45 \div 15$ c) $12 \div -4$

d) $43 \div -10$ e) $(-36 \div 12) \div -3$ f) $-36 \div (12 \div -3)$

9.2 Substituting directed numbers

4 Given that $x = -10$, find the value of:

a) $2x$ b) $-x$ c) $-5x$ d) $x + 4$ e) $x - 2$

f) $2x + 1$ g) $2 - x$ h) $-3 - x$ i) $-10 - x$

5 Given that $y = -15$, find the value of:

a) $10 - y$ b) $(y + 6)^2$ c) $(y - 5)^2$ d) $\dfrac{y}{3}$ e) $-\dfrac{1}{5}y$

f) $\dfrac{y-5}{2}$ g) $\dfrac{y+25}{y+5}$ h) $\dfrac{y-1}{y+7}$ i) $\left(\dfrac{y-3}{6}\right)^2$

6 Find the value of these expressions given that $p = 4$ and $q = -20$:

a) pq b) $p + q$ c) $p - q$ d) $\dfrac{q}{p}$ e) $\dfrac{p^2}{2}$

f) $\left(\dfrac{p}{2}\right)^2$ g) $3p - q$ h) $q - 3p$ i) $-(q - 3p)^2$

7 Given that $C = \frac{5}{9}(F - 32)$, use a calculator to find the value of C correct to 3 S.F. when F is:

a) 87   b) 46   c) -18 d) 417

9.3 Solving equations

8   Find the values of x given in these flow diagrams:

a) $x \rightarrow \boxed{\times 11} \rightarrow \boxed{-19} \rightarrow 80$

b) $x \rightarrow \boxed{\div 10} \rightarrow \boxed{+25} \rightarrow 37$

c) $x \rightarrow \boxed{-21} \rightarrow \boxed{\times 15} \rightarrow 60$

d) $x \rightarrow \boxed{+124} \rightarrow \boxed{\div 8} \rightarrow 17$

9   Draw flow diagrams for these equations and solve them by reversing the process:

a) $3x - 1 = 17$ b) $3(x - 1) = 24$ c) $\dfrac{x}{4} + 7 = 12$

d) $\dfrac{2x}{3} + 11 = 23$ e) $\dfrac{5}{4}(x - 9) = 25$ f) $\dfrac{4x + 3}{5} = 7$

10   Use flow diagrams to solve these equations:

a) $\sqrt{\dfrac{x - 8}{3}} = 5$ b) $\dfrac{\sqrt{x} + 7}{4} = 6$ c) $\dfrac{\sqrt{x + 23}}{2} = 5$

d) $3x^2 + 1 = 49$ e) $(x + 3)^2 = 25$ f) $2x^3 + 100 = -28$

11   a)

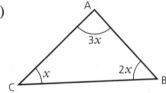

Find the size of angle ABC.

b)

The diagram shows a rectangular enclosure made from 24 m of fencing. What is the area of the enclosure?

12   Let $x = 0.4\dot{7}\dot{1}$. Write as decimals: a) $10x$ b) $1000x$.
Use your answers to write x as a fraction.

9.4 Sequences

13   Write down the next two terms in each of these sequences:

a) $10, 17, 24, 31, \ldots \ldots$ b) $45, 35, 25, 15, \ldots \ldots$
c) $-9, -3, 3, 9, \ldots \ldots$ d) $16, 8, 4, 2, \ldots \ldots$

14   List the first five terms of the sequences defined by:

a) $u_n = 3n - 1$ b) $u_n = 2n + 5$ c) $u_n = (n - 1)(n + 1)$ d) $u_n = n^3$

15   The triangle numbers are defined by $u_n = \dfrac{n}{2}(n + 1)$. Find the value of:

a) the 10th   b) the 50th   c) the 1000th triangle number.

16 The diagrams show the first 3 **square numbers**.

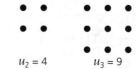

a) Copy and complete the pattern to show the first 10 square numbers.

b) Find the values of u_{12}, u_{20}.

c) Find an expression for u_n.

$u_1 = 1$ $u_2 = 4$ $u_3 = 9$

17 These diagrams show how the pattern can be built up by adding extra dots. In each case, the enclosed

dots represent the **differences** between the square numbers.

a) List the differences for the first ten square numbers.

b) Find the value of $1 + 3 + 5 + 7 + 9$.

c) Find the sum of the first ten odd numbers.

d) Find the sum of the first 100 odd numbers.

e) Find the sum of the first n odd numbers.

PROBABILITY (2)

In situations where all the outcomes have an equal chance:

$$\text{probability of an event} = \frac{\text{number of ways that event can happen}}{\text{total number of different outcomes}}$$

■ Probability of an event which is certain $= 1$
■ Probability of an event which is impossible $= 0$
■ Probability that an event does not happen $=$

  $1 -$ probability that it does happen

Example
There are 24 cans of drink on a cardboard tray. 18 of the cans are cola and 6 are lemonade. If I pick a can at random, what is the probability that it is:
a) a can of lemonade
b) not a can of lemonade
c) a can of orangeade?

Answer
a) Probability (can is lemonade) $= \frac{6}{24} = \frac{1}{4}$

b) Probability (can is not lemonade) $= \frac{18}{24} = \frac{3}{4}$

  Alternatively use:
  Probability (can is not lemonade) $= 1 -$ probability (can is lemonade)
  $= 1 - \frac{1}{4} = \frac{3}{4}$

c) Probability (can is orangeade) $= 0$

Combined events

If a coin and a dice are thrown together there are 12 possible outcomes. These can be shown by a diagram:

Each of these 12 outcomes is equally likely, so the probability of H, 5 is $\frac{1}{12}$. The probability of tails and an odd number is $\frac{3}{12}$ or $\frac{1}{4}$.

| | Coin | |
	Heads	Tails
1	H, 1	T, 1
2	H, 2	T, 2
3	H, 3	T, 3
4	H, 4	T, 4
5	H, 5	T, 5
6	H, 6	T, 6

Score on dice

A useful rule is:

The total number of outcomes can be found by multiplying the number of outcomes for the first event by the number of outcomes for the second event.

Example

If a four-sided dice and a six-sided dice are thrown together, how many outcomes are possible?

Answer

$4 \times 6 = 24$

Questions

10.1 to 10.2 Probability problems

1   A bag contains 3 banana toffees, 2 mint toffees and 4 strawberry toffees. If I take a toffee without looking, what is the probability that:
   a) it is a banana toffee
   b) it is banana or mint
   c) it is banana or mint or strawberry
   d) it is a liquorice toffee?

2   A letter is picked at random from the English alphabet. Find the probability that:
   a) the letter is a vowel
   b) the letter is *not* a vowel
   c) the letter is one which appears in the word MATHEMATICS
   d) the letter comes from the second half of the alphabet.

3   A drawer contains black socks and white socks. If a sock is picked out at random the probability that it is black is $\frac{4}{9}$.
   a) What is the probability of picking a white sock?
   b) If there are 12 black socks in the drawer, how many white ones are there?

4   A box contains yellow, red and green counters. A counter is picked out at random.
   a) If the probability of picking a yellow counter is $\frac{1}{10}$ and the probability of picking a red one is $\frac{3}{5}$, what is the probability of getting a green one?
   b) Which colour are there most of?

5   I have 12 cards in my hand. I ask my partner to pick one (without looking). The probability that she picks an ace is $\frac{1}{6}$. How many aces are there in my hand?

6   In a car park there is a probability of $\frac{2}{5}$ that a car picked at random is British. There are 90 foreign cars in the car park. How many British cars are there?

10.3 Probability games

7 Shake two coins in a plastic cup and turn them out onto a table. Record your result onto a chart like this:

Result	Tally	Frequency
2 heads		
one of each		
2 tails		

a) If you repeat the experiment 24 times in all, how many of each result do you expect to get (roughly)?

b) Repeat the experiment 24 times and compare your results to your answer to question **a)**.

c) Here is a diagram to show all the possible results of this experiment. Copy the diagram and fill in the missing results.

d) How many possible outcomes are there?

e) What is the probability of throwing two heads?

f) What is the probability of throwing one head and one tail in any order?

g) What is the probability of throwing two tails?

h) What is the probability of throwing at least one head?

i) Explain why your answers to questions **f)** and **g)** have a total of 1.

First coin

	H	T
Second coin H	H, H	?
Second coin T	?	?

8 a) Draw a table like this in which to record all the possible results of throwing a six-sided dice and a four-sided dice together.

		6-sided dice					
		1	2	3	4	5	6
4-sided dice	1						7
	2		4	5			
	3						
	4						

b) Your score is the TOTAL for the two dice. Fill in the totals on the table.

c) What is the probability of scoring a total of 1?

d) What is the probability of scoring a total of 2?

e) What is the probability of scoring a total of 4?

f) What is the probability of scoring a total of 5?

10.4 Payoffs

9   Rachel decides to organise a game for the school Autumn Fair using raffle tickets. She rolls up each raffle ticket and places it inside a drinking straw. Anyone wishing to play the game must pay 10p to pick a straw. If the number on the ticket inside their straw contains a figure '7' they win a prize.

a) Rachel has the tickets 001 to 300 available. How much money will she take in if she is able to sell all 300 numbers?

b) How many of the straws will contain winning numbers?

c) How much prize money will she have to pay out if she pays 50p for a single figure 7 and a star prize of £1 for two sevens on the same ticket?

d) How much profit will she make?

e) What is the probability that a player will win 50p?

f) What is the probability that a player will win £1?

10   Lamia and Joe set up a game of 'shove penny' (described in Unit 4). The probability that a player wins by pushing their penny so that it lies completely inside a square is $\frac{1}{4}$. Lamia decides to charge people 10p to play.

a) If 200 people play this game, how much money will Lamia and Joe collect?

b) How many people are likely to win prizes?

c) Joe hopes that they can make a profit of £10 during the afternoon. How much can they afford to give prize winners in order to stand a reasonable chance of making that amount of profit?

11   In David's form there are five pupils, David, Sally, Nathan, Karim and Martha, who all want to be in their team for the Interform pop quiz. There are only three people in a team.

They decide that the one fair way to choose is to use raffle tickets. How many different teams can be chosen? Here are some to start you thinking.

David Sally Nathan
David Sally Karim
David Sally Martha
David Nathan Karim

a) List all the possible teams.

b) In how many teams is David chosen?

c) In how many teams is David not chosen?

d) What is the probability that David will be chosen?

e) What is the probability that David and Karim are chosen together?

f) What is the probability that Sally and Martha are chosen together?

g) What is the probability that neither Sally nor Martha are chosen?

STRAIGHT LINES

Ratios

> A ratio provides a means of comparing two related quantities.

For every turn of the pedals of a particular bicycle, the wheels make three complete turns. This relationship can be described by the ratio (called the **gear ratio**) which is $1:3$.

read as 1 to 3

Ratios are closely related to fractions and obey the same rules for finding equivalent forms.

For example, the fraction $\frac{10}{15}$ may be simplified by cancelling a common factor of 5 to become $\frac{2}{3}$.

In the same way, the ratio $10:15$ can be simplified to $2:3$.

The simplification of some ratios may involve the conversion, and cancelling, of units.

For example:

$$£3.60:90p \;=\; 360p:90p \;=\; 360:90 \;=\; 4:1$$
$$75\text{ cm}:4\text{ m} \;=\; 75\text{ cm}:400\text{ cm} \;=\; 75:400 \;=\; 3:16$$

Gradient

The gradient of a line is a measure of its slope, or steepness, and depends on the **ratio** of the vertical change to the horizontal.

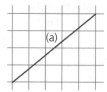
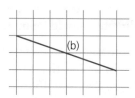

Gradient of line **(a)** is $\frac{4}{5}$.   Gradient of line **(b)** is $-\frac{1}{3}$.

Suppose the coordinates of points A and B are (x_A, y_A) and (x_B, y_B).

Then the gradient of a line through A and B can be calculated directly using:

$$\frac{y_B - y_A}{x_B - x_A}$$

Equations of lines

The equation of a line is simply a statement, given in terms of coordinates, that describes the special nature of those points that lie on the line.

The diagrams show examples of the lines and equations studied so far.

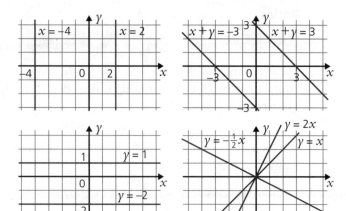

Questions

11.1 Using ratios

1 The US nickel is made up of 25% nickel and 75% copper. What is the ratio of:
a) nickel to copper
b) copper to nickel?

2 The cooling system of a car contains water and antifreeze in the ratio 2:1. Find the total amount of fluid in the system if it contains:
a) 4 pints of antifreeze
b) 9 pints of water.

3 A blend of tea is made from Darjeeling and China teas in the ratio 2:5.
a) How much China tea is needed to mix with 240 g of Darjeeling tea?
b) How much Darjeeling tea should be mixed with 450 g of China tea?

4 Find the missing values in these statements:
a) $5:4 = 15:?$
b) $3:7 = 15:?$
c) $4:9 = ?:18$
d) $25:30 = 5:?$
e) $25:30 = 15:?$
f) $24:36 = 10:?$
g) $12:? = 48:36$
h) $?:100 = 7.3:10$
i) $10:49 = 1:?$

5 Write these ratios in their simplest form:
a) $24:48$
b) $25:75$
c) $25:30$
d) $0.7:0.35$
e) $0.03:0.007$
f) $\frac{3}{11} : \frac{7}{11}$
g) $70\,\text{cm}:1\,\text{m}$
h) $£4.50:50\text{p}$
i) $500\,\text{g}:3\,\text{kg}$
j) $45\,\text{minutes}:1\,\text{hour}$
k) $8\,\text{inches}:2\,\text{feet}$
l) $400\,\text{m}:1\,\text{km}$

6 Write these ratios in the form $1:n$:
a) $10:50$
b) $10:23$
c) $100:47$
d) $5:6$
e) $5\,\text{minutes}:5\,\text{hours}$
f) $11\,\text{days}:33\,\text{weeks}$

7 This drawing of the Eiffel Tower is drawn to a scale of 1 : 7000. Calculate the height of the tower in metres.

11.2 Gradient

8 Find the gradient of each of the lines shown in the diagram.

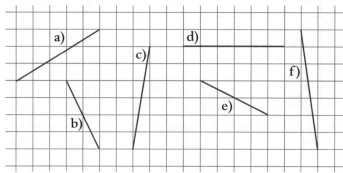

9 Calculate the gradients of the lines joining the following pairs of points. Simplify your answers where possible.

a) $(11, 7)$ and $(5, 3)$ b) $(27.8, 15)$ and $(24.3, 22)$

10 The points A, B and C have coordinates $(1, 8)$, $(4, 13)$ and $(13, 28)$ respectively. Calculate the gradient of:

a) AB b) BC

Explain how the gradient of AC can now be found without further calculation.

11.3 Coordinates in four quadrants

11 State the coordinates of the labelled points.

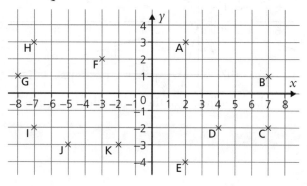

12 Calculate the gradient of the line joining:
   a) $(-7, 6)$ to $(-10, -9)$
   b) $(11, -5)$ to $(-9, -15)$
   c) $(-7, -18)$ to $(23, -28)$

11.4 Equations of lines

13 Write down the equations of the labelled lines.

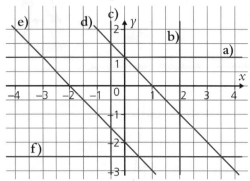

14 Find the coordinates of the point of intersection of the lines with equations:
   a) $x + y = 5$ and $y = 3$
   b) $y = -2$ and $x = 8$
   c) $x = 11.9$ and $y = -4$
   d) $x = -2.5$ and $x + y = 10$

15 Using axes labelled from -6 to 6, draw the graphs of the following equations. Write the equation next to the graph in each case.
   a) $x = 4$ **b)** $x + y = 3$ **c)** $y = -3.5$

16 Write down the equation of each of these lines.

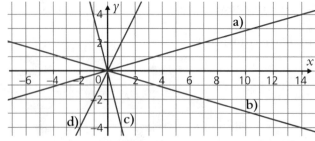

17 Give the coordinates of the point where the line $x = 5$ meets the line $y = 4x$.

BEARINGS AND PLANS

Bearings

One way of describing direction is to refer to the points of the compass.

Here are the principal points of the compass.

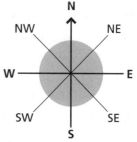

Another way of describing direction is to give a **bearing**. A bearing is an angle measured in a clockwise direction from North. It gives the direction for a journey between two places. A bearing is always an angle between 0° and 360° and is written as a three-figure number.

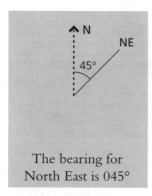

The bearing for North East is 045°

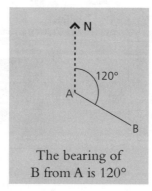

The bearing of B from A is 120°

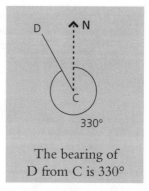

The bearing of D from C is 330°

Back bearings give directions for the return journey. They can always be calculated using alternate angles and parallel lines.

Example

If the bearing of A from O is 030°, what is the bearing of O from A (the back bearing)?

Answer
To find the answer first draw in another North line at A.

The two lines pointing North are parallel lines. This means that we can find that OAS is also 30° using alternate angles.

The bearing of O from A must be 180° + 30° = 210°.

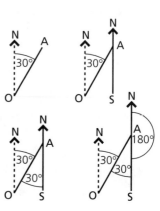

Plans and elevations

A **plan** is the outline shape of an object viewed from above.

A side or front view of a building (or object) is called an **elevation**.
A front view is called a front elevation.
A side view is called a side elevation.

Here are the plan and the elevations of a garage and lean-to shed.

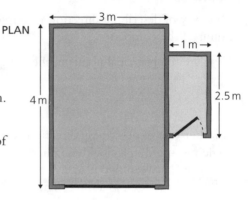

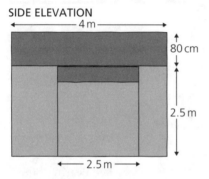

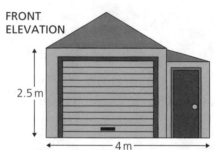

Questions

12.1 to 12.3 Bearings, back bearings and scale drawings

1 **a)** Draw sketches to show each of the following bearings:
    (i) 250°   (ii) 055°   (iii) 305°   (iv) 135°   (v) 295°

  b) For each of the bearings above, give the back bearing which would return you to your starting point.

2 For each of the diagrams below give the bearing of **a)** OX, **b)** XO.

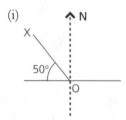
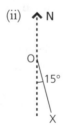
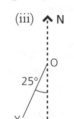
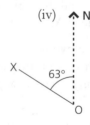

3 Mark a point L in the middle of your page. This represents a lighthouse on a rock.
Draw in a dotted line to show the direction of North.
Ship A is 5.1 km away from the lighthouse on a bearing of 035°.
Use a scale of 1 cm to 1 km to show the position of ship A on your diagram.

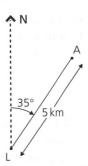

4 Mark the positions of these ships on your question 3 diagram.
   a) Which two ships are closest together? Find the distance between them.
   b) Which two ships are furthest apart? Find the distance between them.

Ship	Bearing from L	Distance from L
B	100°	2.4 km
C	145°	3.6 km
D	207°	4.8 km
E	310°	1.7 km

5 Mark two points X and Y near the centre of a page, 5 cm apart. These points stand for two coastguard stations 20 km apart.
   a) What scale are you using here? Is it:
   (i) 1 : 4 (ii) 1 : 400 (iii) 1 : 4000
   (iv) 1 : 400 000?
   b) Draw in North lines at X and Y. A ship in distress is on a bearing of 050° from X and 322° from Y. Fix its position on your diagram.
   c) Find the distances of the ship from X and Y.

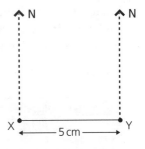

12.4 to 12.5 Plans, elevations and scale drawings

6 Look at the plan and elevations for the garage and lean-to shed opposite.
   a) The builder has plans showing this building which use a scale of 5 cm to 1 m.
   Is this:
   (i) 1 : 50 (ii) 1 : 5 (iii) 1 : 20 (iv) 1 : 200 ?
   b) Find the total floor area of the garage and shed combined.
   c) What is the area of the back wall of the garage?
   d) Express the floor area of the shed as a percentage of the total floor area.

7 Draw an accurate plan of your ideal bedroom showing all the furniture accurately drawn. Include pictures of the furniture if you wish, but do not stick them on to the actual plan.

8   This is a sketch showing
the plan of a kitchen. The
kitchen measures 2.6 m by
4 m. Both doors are 80 cm
wide. There is a built-in
unit going right across
the end of the room under
the window. This includes
sink and worktops with
cupboards underneath.

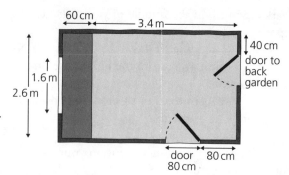

a) Make a scale drawing of the plan using a scale of 1 : 20.

b) Cut out plans of the following items of furniture to the same scale.

Refrigerator	60 cm	by 60 cm
Cooker	55 cm	by 55 cm
Washing machine	60 cm	by 60 cm
Small table	85 cm	by 50 cm
Cupboard	100 cm	by 55 cm

Arrange these on your plan, in a sensible way. Ensure that all the cupboards
can be opened, particularly those in the unit under the window. Draw the
items onto your plan when you have decided on their final positions.

9   The diagrams show elevations of all the walls in a living room.

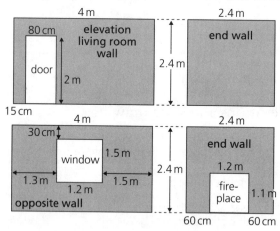

The walls (not the ceiling) are to be papered using striped wallpaper (no
design to match). Each roll of paper is 50 cm wide.

a) What is the combined width of 2 pieces of wallpaper?
4 pieces? 6 pieces?

b) Each roll contains 10.5 metres of wallpaper. Use the elevations to work out
how many rolls of paper to buy.

ALGEBRA AND GRAPHS (1)

Removing brackets

$a + (b + c) = a + b + c$ *When the sign outside the brackets is a '+', the signs of terms*
$a + (b - c) = a + b - c$ *inside the brackets are unchanged on removing the brackets.*

$a - (b + c) = a - b - c$ *However, a '−' sign outside the brackets has the effect of*
$a - (b - c) = a - b + c$ *changing all the signs inside as the brackets are removed.*

$a(b + c) = ab + ac$ *The rule for multiplying out brackets, also known as*
$a(b + c + d) = ab + ac + ad$ *__expanding__ brackets, may be extended to any number of terms.*

For example:
$5x + 3(x - 2) = 5x + 3x - 6 = 8x - 6$
$3 - 2(x - 4) = 3 - 2x + 8 = 11 - 2x$

Factorising

The process of factorising is the reverse process of multiplying out brackets
and involves:
(i)   taking any common factors outside the brackets
(ii)   completing the factor, inside the brackets, to make the factorised form
     equivalent to the original expression.

For example:
$5y + 10 = 5(y + 2)$ $5xy - 10x = 5x(y - 2)$ $\pi r^2 l - \pi r^3 = \pi r^2(l - r)$

Gradient intercept form

The graph of any equation of the form $y = mx + c$, where m and c are
constants, is a straight line.

The value of m gives the gradient of the line and the y-intercept is given by c.
For example, the graph of the equation $y = 3x - 5$ is a straight line with
gradient 3, crossing the y-axis at −5.

Quadratics

The equation $y = x^2$ is an example of a different form of equation known as a
quadratic. In a quadratic expression in x, the highest power of x is 2 and its
most general form is $ax^2 + bx + c$, where a, b, and c are constants. The
following expressions are quadratics.

$2x^2 - 3$ $(a = 2, b = 0$ and $c = -3)$

$x^2 + 0.3x$ $(a = 1, b = 0.3$ and $c = 0)$

The graph of a quadratic is not a straight line but a special curve called
a **parabola.**

When $a > 0$,
the graph
looks like this.

When $a < 0$,
the graph
looks like this.

Questions

13.1 Removing brackets

1 Remove the brackets from these expressions:
a) $2x + (3y - z)$ **b)** $3q - (4p + r)$ **c)** $-(3l - 2m + 4n)$
d) $(w + 2x) + (3y - z)$ **e)** $(2p - 5q) - (3r - 4s)$ **f)** $3a - (b + 2c - 7d)$

2 Remove the brackets and simplify:
a) $4x + (5 - 2x)$ **b)** $7 - (6y - 3)$ **c)** $3p - 5q - (p - 5q)$
d) $a - 2b + (3a - b)$ **e)** $(2x - 3) - (4 - 3x)$ **f)** $8 + (6 - 3y) - (y + 4)$

3 Find, and simplify, expressions for the perimeters of these figures.

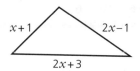 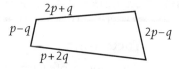

4 Expand:
a) $5(x + 4)$ **b)** $3(2x - 1)$ **c)** $x(x + 3)$
d) $y(3y - 2)$ **e)** $-x(3x - y)$ **f)** $xy(x + y + 1)$

5 Expand and simplify:
a) $2(x + 3) + 3(x + 2)$ **b)** $5y - 3(y - 2)$ **c)** $3x + 1 + 4(2x + 3)$
d) $x - 3z - 2(4 - x + z)$ **e)** $3(x^2 + 5) - (x^2 - 4)$ **f)** $x(4x + 3) - 3(x^2 + 1)$

13.2 Factorising

6 Copy and complete:
a) $12x + 6y = 6(... + ...)$ **b)** $4x - 6xy = 2x(... - ...)$ **c)** $8pq - 12q = ...(... - 3)$
d) $x^2y + xy^3 = xy(... + ...)$ **e)** $x^2y - x^2y^2 = x^2y(... - ...)$ **f)** $\pi ab^2 + ... = \pi ab(... + a)$

7 Factorise fully, i.e. take out the largest common factor in each case:
a) $xy + 5x$ **b)** $9lm + 12m^2$ **c)** $2\pi r^2 - 3\pi rh$
d) $pqr + pq - pr$ **e)** $15ab - 10a^2 + 5ab^2$ **f)** $27x^3y + 18x^2y - 36xy$

8 Simplify these expressions and leave your answers in factorised form:
a) $3h + 2k + 9h + 7 + 4k + 11$ **b)** $3(m + 2n + 1) - (3 - 5m - 2n)$
c) $2(3x + 2y - z) + 4(x - 2y) - 6(y + 3z)$ **d)** $x(3x - 4) + 5(x^2 + 3) - (x^2 - 4x + 1)$
e) $3(x + 2y) + 7(x + 2y)$ **f)** $11(3m + 4n - 6) - 5(3m + 4n - 6)$

13.3 Gradient intercept form

9 Find the gradient and y-intercept of each of the lines labelled in the diagram. Hence write down the equation of each line.

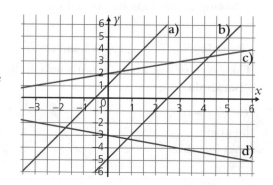

10 Which of the following points does the line $y = 2x - 3$ contain?
a) $(4, 1)$ b) $(0, -3)$ c) $(8, 19)$ d) $(-2, -7)$

11 Copy and complete the following coordinates so that the points lie on the line $y = 0.5x + 1$.
a) $(10, ...)$ b) $(-10, ...)$ c) $(0, ...)$ d) $(7, ...)$
e) $(11, ...)$ f) $(-3, ...)$ g) $(..., 7)$ h) $(..., 0)$

12 Write down the equation of the line, parallel to the line $y = 3x + 9$, which passes through the point with coordinates $(0, 2.5)$. Show that the point $(1.5, 7)$ lies on this line.

13 Find the coordinates of the points where the following lines meet the line $y = 4x - 5$. Make your method clear in each case.
a) $x = 6$ b) $x = 0$ c) $x = -1$ d) $y = 3$

14 Write the following equations in the form $y = mx + c$. Hence find the gradient and y-intercept in each case.
a) $y = 3(x - 4)$ b) $y = 2x + 4(x + 5)$
c) $y = 7x + 3 + (5 - 3x)$ d) $y = 3x - 2 - (5x - 6)$

15 The coordinates of A and B are $(3, 1)$ and $(5, 9)$ respectively. Find the equation of the line parallel to AB which passes through $(0, -7.8)$.

13.4 Using graphs to solve equations

16 Use the diagram to find the solutions of these equations:
a) $0.6x - 0.5 = 1$
b) $0.6x - 0.5 = 1.5$

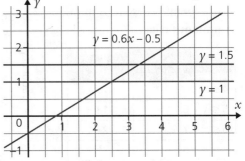

17 Find the value of $1.2x + 3.7$ when $x = 0$ and when $x = 5$. Explain how this shows that the equation $1.2x + 3.7 = 8$ has a solution between 0 and 5.
Draw the graphs of $y = 1.2x + 3.7$ and $y = 8$ for $0 \leq x \leq 5$.
Use the graphs to solve $1.2x + 3.7 = 8$ correct to 1 decimal place.

18 The diagram shows a sketch of the graph of $y = x^2 + 3x$.
a) How many solutions are there to the equation $x^2 + 3x = 0$?
b) Explain how you were able to decide and state the values of x.
c) Will the equation $x^2 + 3x = a$ have the same number of solutions for any value of a? Explain your answer by copying the sketch and drawing some extra lines.

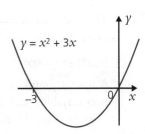

CHARTS, GRAPHS, HISTOGRAMS

Types of variable

Type of variable	Obtained by	Useful graphs
categorical data or groups	classifying (e.g. what colour?)	pie charts for proportions bar chart for frequencies
discrete data	counting (e.g. how many brothers and sisters?)	bar line graph for frequencies (pie chart for proportions)
continuous data	measuring (e.g. how long? how heavy?)	histogram (pie chart for proportions)

Histograms

A histogram is drawn to illustrate continuous data.

Ages of children at infant school	Frequency
$4 \leq x < 5$	5
$5 \leq x < 6$	18
$6 \leq x < 7$	27
$7 \leq x < 8$	25

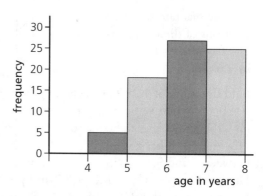

(Note that age is a continuous variable, not discrete as it may first appear.)

There should be no gaps between the blocks on the histogram, and the height of the block represents the frequency for each group.

Scatter graphs

A scatter graph can be drawn to investigate a possible relationship between two variables (height and weight, for example). The data must be collected in pairs and may be either discrete or continuous.

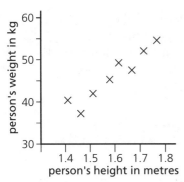

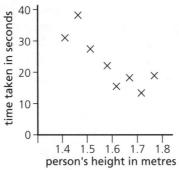

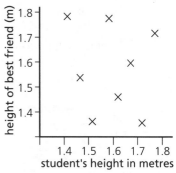

This scatter graph shows a *positive* correlation between a person's height and weight. Both variables increase together. (The trend is upwards to the right.)

This scatter graph shows a *negative* correlation between a person's height and the time taken to run 200 metres. As height increases, time decreases. (The trend is downwards to the right.)

If two variables are unrelated, such as a year 10 student's height and the height of his best friend, the scatter graph shows a random scatter of points indicating a zero or very low correlation.

Questions

14.1 to 14.4 Way of representing data

1   For each variable listed below decide which diagram would be most suitable. Choose from pie chart, bar chart, bar line graph and histogram.
   a) heights of students
   b) proportion of income spent on rent, food, clothes, fares and entertainment
   c) number of teeth with fillings
   d) proportion of lessons spent on each school subject
   e) weights of new-born babies
   f) number of buses per day on each bus route
   g) colour of hair
   h) blood group
   i) time taken to travel to school
   j) ages of people passing their driving test

2   Draw a pie chart to show the nutritional composition of a packet of crisps, as listed here. One of the calculations has been done for you.

Nutritional element	Weight	Angle in pie chart
protein	1.4 g	
carbohydrate	12.0 g	
fat	9.2 g	
fibre	1.1 g	
sodium	0.3 g	$\frac{0.3}{24} \times 360 = 4.5°$
	TOTAL	TOTAL

3   Ramesh has conducted a survey among students in year 10 and also among
    pupils in a year 6 class at the local junior school. Using a street map he has
    located each person's address and worked out how far their journey is to school.
    He has drawn two histograms to illustrate his data, but has not identified
    which histogram belongs to which group of pupils.

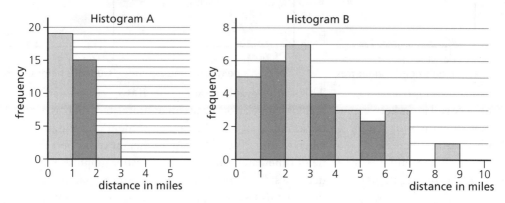

a) For each histogram find the modal class and the range.
b) Which histogram illustrates year 6 results and which illustrates year 10?

4   Sally decides to conduct a survey into supermarket shopping as a coursework
    project. She times how long each of 25 customers had to wait in the
    check-out queues. She can obtain an exact time by recording the time they
    arrive in the queue and comparing this with the time recorded on the
    check-out receipt. Here are the results:

Supermarket survey – check-out queuing times

2 min 25 s	3 min 56 s	2 min 47 s	4 min 3 s	3 min 27 s
3 min 18 s	5 min 10 s	4 min 8 s	3 min 29 s	2 min 56 s
4 min 35 s	4 min 16 s	4 min 33 s	5 min	3 min 38 s
3 min 49 s	3 min 14 s	2 min 58 s	4 min 16 s	3 min 35 s
4 min 40 s	2 min 29 s	4 min 51 s	3 min 49 s	

Organise the results into a frequency
table using the following groupings:

a) Explain what is meant by
   2 min ≤ x < 2 min 30 s.
b) Draw a histogram (frequency graph)
   for these check-out queuing times.
c) What is the modal class (class or
   interval with the highest frequency)
   for waiting times?

Waiting time	Tally	Frequency
2 min ≤ x < 2 min 30 s		
2 min 30 s ≤ x < 3 min		
3 min ≤ x < 3 min 30 s		
3 min 30 s ≤ x < 4 min		
4 min ≤ x < 4 min 30 s		
4 min 30 s ≤ x < 5 min		
5 min ≤ x < 5 min 30 s		

d) Sally conducted her survey on a Saturday morning. Do you think she would
   have obtained similar results on a Tuesday morning? Explain your answer.

14.5 to 14.6 Scatter graphs and correlations

5   Joe conducted a survey at his local barber's shop. He asked the customers their ages and also how many times they had been to the barber in the past six months.

Age	51	56	18	48	26	33	59	66	45	38	24	16	58	23	39
Number of visits to barber	3	4	7	4	6	3	2	1	4	4	7	8	2	6	4

a) Draw a scatter graph to illustrate Joe's barber-shop results. Show age on the horizontal axis and number of visits to the barber's shop on the vertical axis.

b) Is there any relationship between the age of the customer and the frequency with which he visits the barber? Explain in your own words what the graph shows.

c) Can you describe this as a positive correlation, negative correlation or zero correlation?

6   Sally asks her family if they will allow her to weigh them and measure their heights. This is what she found:

Height (cm)	140	132	164	169	157	185	176	143
Weight (kg)	38	29	60	57	55	73	68	41

a) Draw a scatter graph with height on the horizontal axis and weight on the vertical axis, then plot Sally's results.

b) Is there a strong correlation between height and weight? Is this positive or negative?

c) Were all of the people in Sally's sample adults? Explain your answer.

d) If Sally's sample had included *only* adults, would she have found a positive relationship between height and weight?

15 RATIO, PERCENTAGE, PROPORTION

Division in a given ratio

Example

Share £360 between A, B and C in the ratio 5 : 3 : 2.

Answer

Regard the amount as being divided into $5 + 3 + 2 = 10$ parts.

£360 ÷ 10 = £36 (i.e. $\frac{1}{10}$ of £360 = £36)

A receives $\frac{5}{10}$ of £360 = $5 \times$ £36 = £180.

(Alternatively, $\frac{5}{10} = \frac{1}{2}$ and $\frac{1}{2}$ of £360 = £180.)

In the same way, B receives $3 \times$ £36 = £108 and C receives $2 \times$ £36 = £72.

Check: $180 + 108 + 72 = 360$.

Ratio and percentage

Example

The mathematics department in a school spends money on books and equipment in the ratio 4 : 1. Express the amount spent on books as a percentage of the total.

Answer

Step 1 Express the given amount as a *fraction* of the total.

Amount spent on books is $\frac{4}{5}$ of total.

Step 2 Convert the fraction to a percentage by multiplying by 100.

$\frac{4}{5} \times 100 = 80\%$

Therefore 80% of the money is spent on books.

(*Note*: if the ratio in the example was, say, 11 : 3 then the calculation would become $\frac{11}{14} \times 100$. Using a calculator, this may be worked out as

11 [÷] 14 [×] 100

giving 78.6% to 1 D.P.)

One amount as a percentage of another

To express an amount (A) as a percentage of another amount (B), use:

$\frac{A}{B} \times 100\%$

A very useful result concerns the idea of **percentage change** which is given by:

$$\text{percentage change} = \frac{\text{change in value}}{\text{original value}} \times 100\%$$

Proportion

Whenever two variables remain in constant ratio to each other they are said to be **proportional**.

Example

The cost of a particular kind of rug is proportional to its area. If a rug of area 2.1 m² costs £30 find the cost of a rug of area **a)** 8.4 m², **b)** 15 m².

Answer

a) $\frac{\text{cost}}{\text{area}}$ is constant so $\frac{30}{2.1} = \frac{?}{8.4}$ giving the cost as £30 × 4 = £120.

$\times 4 \ (= \frac{8.4}{2.1})$

b) In the same way, $\frac{30}{2.1} = \frac{?}{15}$.

$\times \frac{15}{2.1}$

The cost can now be worked out as $£30 \times \frac{15}{2.1} = £214.29$.

Alternatively, using the **unitary method**, we could find the cost of 1 m² and then multiply by 15.

Questions

15.1 Division in a given ratio

1 A couple decide to divide their garden into areas of paving, turf and flowers in the ratio 1:3:2.
If the total area of their garden is 300 m², how much of the garden do they plan to use for:
a) paving **b)** turf **c)** flowers?

2 A university student earns £40 per week doing part-time work. If the money is used for food, other expenses and entertainment in the ratio 5:3:2, how much is spent in each category?

3 Lowey, Manch, Luke and Twigg went strawberry picking. They collected a total of 30 lb of strawberries in the ratio 4:5:7:4.
a) How much did they each collect?
b) If the total cost was £24 how should they have split the bill?

15.2 Ratio and percentage

4 An alloy is made from a mixture of gold and a base metal in the ratio 3:11. What percentage of the alloy is gold?

5 The ratio of boys to girls in a year 10 class is 5:6. What percentage of the class do the girls represent to the nearest 1%?

6 The three members of a local band and their manager agree to share any takings in the ratio:

  5:5:5:2

Calculate the manager's share to the nearest 0.1%.

7 A holiday firm carried out a survey of its customers at a particular resort. The survey found that for every 3 people who had a complaint to make there were 28 who were perfectly satisfied. Find, to 1 decimal place, the percentage of the people in the survey who made a complaint.

15.3 Percentage change

8 An exam is marked out of a possible total of 83. Convert the following marks to percentages as whole numbers. If the pass mark is 55%, how many candidates passed the exam?

a) 37 **b)** 79 **c)** 52 **d)** 48 **e)** 20 **f)** 55 **g)** 62 **h)** 81

9 During a tennis match a player serves the ball 237 times. Of these, 143 are valid first serves, and 19 of these are aces.

a) Find the percentage of serves that were valid at the first attempt.

b) What percentage of the serves were aces?

10 During a hockey season, the keeper saves 17 of the 43 penalties awarded to opposing sides. Express the keeper's success rate as a percentage.

The reserve keeper only played in one match but managed to save a penalty despite letting in 11 goals.

Comment on the idea of relying completely on percentages for team selection.

11 Choose a sport in which percentages are used to compare the performances of competitors. Describe the calculations involved in producing the percentage figures and comment upon their value.

15.4 More than 100%!

12 In which of the following situations would it *never* be sensible to consider a percentage greater than 100%:

a) gain in height **b)** loss of weight **c)** population increase
d) discount **e)** exam score **f)** profit?

13 When Sue guessed the age of her maths teacher on his birthday he wasn't very pleased. She guessed at 56 years when the poor chap was only 27 years old. What was her percentage error to the nearest 0.1%?

14 Last year Sam earned £23 450 but after a wage increase she now earns £24 640.

a) Express her new salary as a percentage of last year's salary to 3 significant figures.

b) What is her percentage increase?

15 Rottweiler puppies are very small when they are born but then grow very rapidly. It is not uncommon for them to double their weight each week for the first three weeks. Use this information to calculate the percentage increase in weight of a Rottweiler during this time.

16 Find out about the way that house prices are changing now. Is it a good time to buy a house? Explain your reasoning.

15.5 Proportion

17 A decorator has a contract to paint 17 identical rooms in a hotel. The time taken to complete the first 5 rooms is 43 hours. If the remaining rooms are completed at the same rate, how much more time will it take to complete the work?

The cost of materials for the first 5 rooms is £116. Calculate the total cost of materials for the 17 rooms, to the nearest £5.

18 A marathon runner completes the first 5 miles of the 26.2 mile course in a time of 31.5 minutes. Assuming that the same pace is maintained, what is the total time taken for the race?

19 Kathy and Simon set off on a touring holiday in which they planned to drive 1500 miles. They filled the petrol tank at the start of the journey and after driving 417 miles filled it again with a further 38 litres of petrol at a cost of £21.09.

a) Calculate the amount of petrol needed for the whole journey to the nearest 10 litres.

b) Find the cost of the petrol needed to the nearest £5.

20 While on holiday in America, James buys a selection of CDs for a total of $43.95.

a) Find the equivalent cost in sterling given that the exchange rate is £1 = $1.5547.

b) How much did he save if the same CDs cost a total of £61.80 in the UK?

21 While on a business trip Sarah stopped at two separate garages for petrol on the outward journey. At the Fillybrooks garage she bought 50 litres of petrol for £24.10 and at the Windy Hill garage she bought 38 litres of petrol for £19.57.

a) Which garage offered the best value on the price of petrol?

b) On the return journey, Sarah bought 24 litres of petrol at the Windy Hill garage and a further 60 litres at the Fillybrooks garage. How much did she spend altogether on petrol?

POLYGONS AND CIRCLES

Quadrilaterals

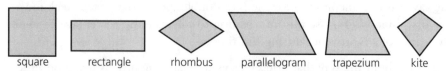

square   rectangle   rhombus   parallelogram   trapezium   kite

Properties of these quadrilaterals are listed here:

	Square	Rectangle	Rhombus	Parallelogram	Trapezium	Kite
All sides equal	✓		✓			
Opposite sides equal	✓	✓	✓	✓		
All angles equal	✓	✓				
Opposite angles equal	✓	✓	✓	✓		(one pair only)
One pair (only) of opposite sides parallel					✓	
Both pairs of opposite sides parallel	✓	✓	✓	✓		
Diagonals equal	✓	✓				
Diagonals bisect each other	✓	✓	✓	✓		
Diagonals perpendicular	✓		✓			✓
Diagonals bisect angles	✓		✓			(one pair only)

The diagram shows the relationships between quadrilaterals.

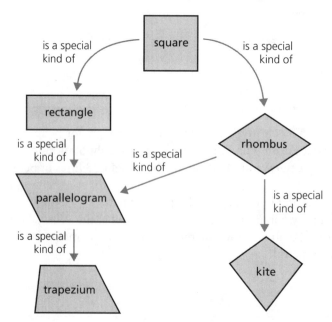

Areas of quadrilaterals

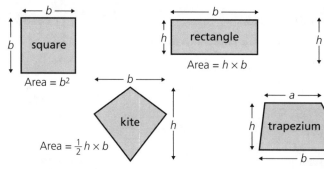

square — Area = b^2

rectangle — Area = $h \times b$

parallelogram — Area = $h \times b$

kite — Area = $\frac{1}{2}h \times b$

trapezium — Area = $\frac{1}{2}(a + b)h$

Polygons

Number of sides	Name
3	Triangle
4	Quadrilateral
5	Pentagon
6	Hexagon
7	Heptagon
8	Octagon
9	Nonagon
10	Decagon
12	Dodecagon

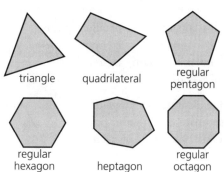

triangle   quadrilateral   regular pentagon

regular hexagon   heptagon   regular octagon

A *regular* polygon has all its sides equal and all its angles equal.

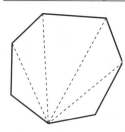

The sum of the **interior angles** of a polygon can be found by dividing it into triangles. Do this by drawing lines (diagonals) from *one* vertex. The number of triangles is always two less than the number of sides.

The sum of the **interior angles** = $180(n - 2)$

The sum of the **exterior angles** of a polygon is always 360°.
$a + b + c + d + e + f + g = 360°$

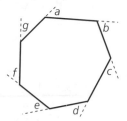

Circles

Circumference = $\pi \times$ diameter
Area = $\pi \times r^2$

The value of π to 3 decimal places is 3.142.

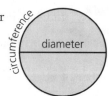

diameter

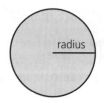

radius

Questions

16.1 and 16.2 Quadrilaterals

1 Decide which of these statements are true and which are false:
a) Some rectangles are squares
b) All squares are rectangles
c) All rectangles are squares
d) All squares are rhombuses
e) All rhombuses are squares
f) Some parallelograms are rhombuses
g) All kites are parallelograms
h) All parallelograms are kites
i) All trapeziums are parallelograms
j) All parallelograms are trapeziums
k) All parallelograms are rectangles
l) All rectangles are parallelograms

2 Make accurate drawings of these quadrilaterals and find the area and perimeter of each.

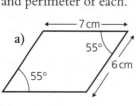
a)

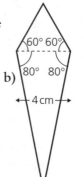
b)

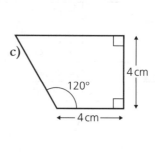
c)

16.3 Polygons

3 Find the sizes of the angles marked with a letter.

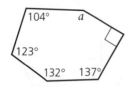

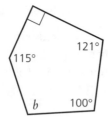

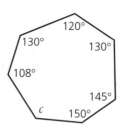

4 An isosceles triangle has one angle of 104°. Find the other two angles.

5 The angles of a triangle are $2x°$, $3x°$ and $4x°$. Find x.

6 a) Is it possible to have a regular polygon with an exterior angle of:
(i) 40° (ii) 50° (iii) 24° ?
b) If it is possible, state the number of sides.

7 The interior angles of a pentagon are $y°$, $(y + 10)°$, $(y + 20)°$, $(y + 40)°$ and $(y + 50)°$. Find y.

8 Is it possible to have a regular polygon with an interior angle of 160°? (*Hint*: what would the exterior angle be?)
If so, how many sides does it have?

9 Is it possible to have a regular polygon with an interior angle of 100°?

16.4 to 16.5 Circles and complex shapes

10 The circumference of a circle of radius 21 cm is approximately:
a) 66 cm   **b)** 1400 cm   **c)** 130 cm   **d)** 1300 cm

11 The area of a circle of radius 6 cm is:
a) $6\pi \text{ cm}^2$ **b)** $72\pi \text{ cm}^2$ **c)** $36\pi \text{ cm}^2$ **d)** $12\pi \text{ cm}^2$

12 Find the area of this ring (called an annulus).
(First find the radii of the outer and inner circles.)

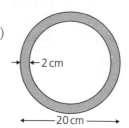

13 This diagram shows a running track which has semicircular ends.

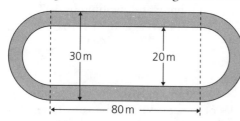

a) Find the outer perimeter of the track.
b) Find the inner perimeter of the track.
c) Find the shaded area.

14 A conveyor belt is driven by a wheel which turns 3 times every second. The radius of the wheel is 1.5 m.

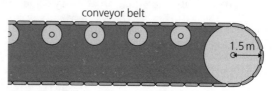

a) Find the circumference of the wheel.
b) How far will the conveyor belt move every second?
c) How far will the conveyor belt move every minute?

NUMBERS AND EQUATIONS

A change of scale

Multiplication by:	Effect	Example
Any number greater than 1	Enlargement	$10 \times 1.6 = 16 \ (16 > 10)$
Any number between zero and 1	Reduction	$10 \times 0.7 = 7 \ \ (7 < 10)$
1	No change	$10 \times 1 = 10$

Division by:	Effect	Example
Any number greater than 1	Reduction	$16 \div 1.6 = 10 \ (10 < 16)$
Any number between zero and 1	Enlargement	$7 \div 0.7 = 10 \ \ (10 > 7)$
1	No change	$10 \div 1 = 10$

Non-calculator methods

When carrying out calculations without a calculator it is useful to be aware that there may be different ways of working towards the result. We can then choose the simplest method to suit a particular situation.

Example (1)

Find 276×99.

Answer

Since $99 = (100 - 1)$ it follows that
$$276 \times 99 = 276(100 - 1)$$
$$= 27\,600 - 276$$
$$= 27\,324$$

Example (2)

What is $3.42 \div 5$?

Answer

For any value of n, $\dfrac{n}{5} = \dfrac{2n}{10}$, which shows that dividing by 5 is the same as doubling and dividing by 10.

Thus $3.42 \div 5 = 6.84 \div 10$
$$= 0.684$$

Balancing equations

An equation such as $3x + 2 = 14$ may be solved by applying the reverse process of the flow-diagram method to both sides of the equation at the same time. The effect is to simplify the equation at every stage until the solution is reached.

Provided that we can recognise the steps of the reverse process, one at a time, the solution can be written simply as:

$$3x + 2 = 14$$
$$3x = 12$$
$$x = 4$$

It is important to balance what we do on both sides of the equation.

This method enables us to solve equations in which the unknown value may appear more than once.

Example (1)

Solve $5x - 7 = 3x + 8$.
Answer

$5x - 7 = 3x + 8$ *By subtracting 3x from both sides, the equation*
$2x - 7 = 8$ *simplifies to one in which x only appears once.*
$2x = 15$
$x = 7.5$

Example (2)

Solve $3(2x - 4) = 9 - 4x$.
Answer

$3(2x - 4) = 9 - 4x$ *A good first step is to remove the brackets.*
$6x - 12 = 9 - 4x$ *Try to keep the number of xs positive so add 4x*
$10x - 12 = 9$ *to both sides rather than subtract 6x.*
$10x = 21$
$x = 2.1$

Questions

17.1 A change of scale

1   Describe the effect of multiplying by each of the following scale factors as
either a reduction or an enlargement:
a) 5   **b)** 0.5   **c)** 0.17   **d)** 1.7

2   Describe the effect of dividing by each of the following as either an
enlargement or a reduction:
a) 1.8   **b)** 0.18   **c)** 1.02   **d)** 0.93

3   Copy and complete the following statements by inserting $<$ or $>$ as appropriate:
a) $12.6 \times 0.87 \dots 12.6$ **b)** $0.63 \times 0.94 \dots 0.63$ **c)** $0.63 \div 0.94 \dots 0.63$
d) $1.38 \times 0.64 \dots 0.64$ **e)** $1.38 \times 0.64 \dots 1.38$ **f)** $1.38 \div 0.64 \dots 1.38$
g) $0.47 \div 2.3 \dots 0.47$ **h)** $2.3 \div 0.47 \dots 2.3$ **i)** $2.3 \times 0.47 \dots 2.3$

4   Without using a calculator, decide which of the following statements
must be false:
a) $4.78 \times 1.08 = 5.1624$ **b)** $3.6456 \div 0.98 = 3.72$ **c)** $0.86 \times 0.75 = 0.8645$
d) $0.645 \div 0.75 = 0.86$ **e)** $1.08 \div 0.97 = 1.0476$ **f)** $1.03 \times 1.4 = 1.342$

17.2 Non–calculator methods

5   Describe a simple way of adding 98 to any number.

6   Add 98 to each of these:
a) 68   **b)** 364   **c)** 197   **d)** 3528

7   Describe a simple way of subtracting 9.9 from any number.

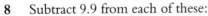

8   Subtract 9.9 from each of these:
    a) 25   **b)** 58   **c)** 253   **d)** 376.4

9   Find the value of each of the following. Show your working in each case:
    a) 85×99 **b)** 347×99 **c)** 842×9.9 **d)** 39×0.99

10   Show your working for these calculations:
    a) 36×200 **b)** 0.74×3000 **c)** $186 \div 30$ **d)** $21 \div 70$
    e) $814 \div 5$ **f)** $2.63 \div 5$ **g)** $8.7 \div 50$ **h)** $12 \div 25$

17.3 Balancing equations

11   Find the solutions of these equations. In each case the answer should be a
positive whole number.
    a) $11x - 23 = 32$ **b)** $5(x - 3) + 7 = 37$ **c)** $16 - (5 - 2x) = 31$

    d) $\dfrac{x}{5} - 3 = 2$ **e)** $\dfrac{x - 5}{3} = 2$ **f)** $\dfrac{2x + 3}{5} + 3 = 10$

    g) $4\sqrt{x} - 7 = 13$ **h)** $3\sqrt{x + 2} = 12$ **i)** $\sqrt{6x + 1} = 5$

12   Solve these. Each answer should be a positive whole number.
    a) $5x + 3 = 2x + 21$ **b)** $4x - 11 = 3x + 9$
    c) $3(x - 5) + 4x = 2x$ **d)** $18 - (7 - 2x) = x + 39$

13   The solutions to the equations given below each contain *one error*. Show by
substituting the given results into the original equations that the answers
are incorrect.
Rewrite the solutions to find the correct answers.
    a) $8x - 6 = 5x + 18$ **b)** $5x - 17 = 16 - 2(6 - x)$
        $3x - 6 = 18$ $5x - 17 = 4 - 2x$
          $3x = 12$ $7x - 17 = 4$
            $x = 4$ $7x = 21$
                         $x = 3$

14   Solve these equations and *check* your answers by substitution. Show all working.
    a) $7x - 3 = 2x + 3$ **b)** $19 - (8 - 3x) = 2x + 9$

    c) $\dfrac{7x - 12}{3} = x$ **d)** $\dfrac{7x - 5}{3} = 2x - 3$

HYPOTHESES

State the hypothesis ① → Decide which data to collect ② → Collect the data ③ → Analyse the data ④ → Interpret the results ⑤ → Report your findings with ⑥ reference to the original hypothesis

A hypothesis can be tested by experiment or by a survey.

Testing a hypothesis by experiment

In an experiment you control the changes in one variable and keep all the other factors constant so that they cannot interfere with the results.

An experiment must be carefully designed to exclude the effect of other variables besides the experimental variable. Uncontrolled variables are a source of **bias**.

Here is a diagram drawn to represent an experiment, in which one tray of lettuce seeds is kept at 10 °C, the other at 25 °C. The hypothesis is that the seeds kept at 25 °C will grow faster.

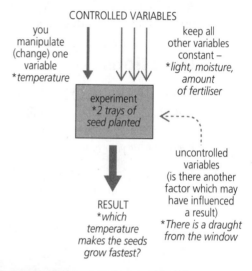

CONTROLLED VARIABLES

you manipulate (change) one variable
*temperature

keep all other variables constant –
*light, moisture, amount of fertiliser

experiment
*2 trays of seed planted

uncontrolled variables
(is there another factor which may have influenced a result)
*There is a draught from the window

RESULT
*which temperature makes the seeds grow fastest?

Guidelines for designing a questionnaire

■ Plan your questionnaire before you start. Ask the questions you need. Miss out the questions you don't need.

■ Keep it simple. Use simple words in short sentences.

■ Avoid questions which suggest the 'right' answer (called *leading questions*).

■ Ask one question at a time.

■ Avoid negatives – they can be confusing.

■ Make sure your questions have a clear meaning. They must be unambiguous. Do not ask vague questions.

■ Avoid embarrassing questions or questions which people will not wish to answer.

■ If you provide boxes for people to tick, make sure every possible answer is provided.

■ Pre-test your questionnaire.

■ Do not ask people to remember events which happened some time ago.

■ Always be polite and thank people for taking part in your survey.

Sources of bias

One of the main sources of bias in both surveys and experiments is the selection of the sample. The sample should be representative of the target population and should (if possible) aim to include all the categories of people in that group. You need to include the various age groups and social backgrounds and both females and males (if these are relevant to your target group).

A survey may also be biased by the wording of the questions(s) asked, the time of day it is conducted and the place.

Questions

18.1 Testing a hypothesis

Collect data from at least 30 people to answer one of questions 1 to 3. Rewrite the question as a hypothesis which you can test. (Alternatively collect data to test a different hypothesis of your own.)

1   Are people's pulse rates higher after exercise?
Decide on a simple exercise such as climbing two flights of stairs.

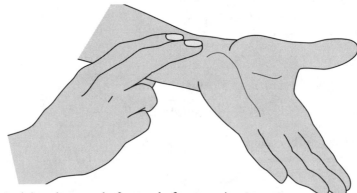

Take people's pulse rates before and after exercise.
WARNING: if anyone experiences difficulty in breathing or chest pain do not allow them to continue.

2   Are parents or pupils more likely to be in favour of school uniform?
Make a two–way table to record your results.

School uniform	Parents	Pupils
In favour		
Not in favour		

Should you choose a sample representing pupils in all age groups? Or should you use pupils in one year group only?

3 Is your writing (or dominant) hand, different in shape from your non-dominant hand?
Which hand do you use for writing?
Which hand makes a bigger 'V' (keeping the fingers stuck together)?

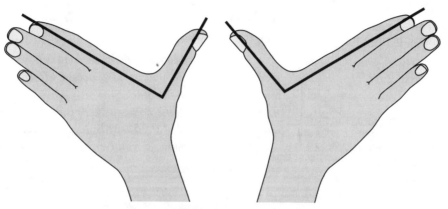

Your results can be recorded on a two-way table like this:

Shape of hand	Right-handed	Left-handed
Right V bigger		
Left V bigger		

18.2 Surveys and questionnaires

You are to carry out a 'split-poll' survey with a partner.
Decide on a topic for your survey.
Do two surveys. Write a report about what you find out.

4 Devise two versions of the same question. One version should be biased, and one unbiased, for example:
(i) Do you think that school uniform gives pupils a sense of identity and should be worn in all schools?
(ii) Are you in favour of pupils wearing a school uniform?
Does the wording of the question affect your results?

5 Use the same question in both surveys but choose different times or days for your two surveys, for example: at 8.30 am before school starts, compared to lunchtime. Does the time of day affect your results?

6 Use the same question in both surveys but go to two different places to conduct your survey, for example: outside a cinema and outside a supermarket (both on a Saturday afternoon).
Does the place affect your results?

19 FRACTIONS AND INEQUALITIES

Scale factors and percentages

The idea of using scale factors to represent an enlargement or a reduction may be applied to the calculation of a percentage increase or decrease.

Example

A pair of running shoes priced at £89.99 is to be reduced by 15% (to the nearest penny) in a sale. Calculate the sale price.

Answer

85% of £89.99 = 0.85 × £89.99
$$= £76.491\ 5$$
$$= £76.49 \text{ (to the nearest penny)}$$

The sale price is £76.49.

Note that when we reduce an amount by 15% we are left with 85% of it.

Since 85% = $\frac{85}{100}$ = 0.85, it follows that 0.85 may be used as a scale factor to reduce any amount by 15%.

Example

A computer is advertised at a price of £998 + VAT. How much would a customer have to pay if the rate of VAT is 17.5%?

Answer

The customer pays 117.5% of £998
$$= 1.175 × £998$$
$$= £1\ 172.65$$

When we increase an amount by 17.5% we then have 117.5% of it.

Since 117.5% = $\frac{117.5}{100}$ = 1.175 it follows that we may use 1.175 as a scale factor to increase any amount by 17.5%.

The diagram below illustrates how the process can be *reversed* in order to find the *original* amount; i.e. to calculate the amount *before* VAT was added divide the total price by 1.175.

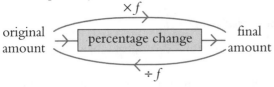

In the example given above, dividing £1 172.65 by 1.175 gives £998 which was the amount before VAT was added.

Solving inequalities

Example

Find the solution, and plot the result on a number line, of:
a) $3x + 2 < 14$ b) $x + 7 \geq 6 - x$

Answer

a) $3x + 2 < 14$
$$3x < 12$$
$$x < 4$$

The steps involved in the solution are the same as those for solving the equation $3x + 2 = 14$. Any value of x less than 4 is a solution.

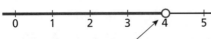

*Note that the end-point is **not** included*

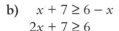
b) $\quad x + 7 \geq 6 - x$ *Add x to both sides. As usual try to keep the number*
$\quad\quad 2x + 7 \geq 6$ *of xs positive.*
$\quad\quad\quad 2x \geq -1$ *Note that $-\frac{1}{2}$ is **included** as a solution.*
$\quad\quad\quad x \geq -\frac{1}{2}$

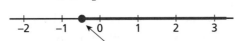

*Note that the end-point **is** included*

Example

Find the integer values of x such that $3 < 2x - 5 \leq 8$.

Answer
$\quad 3 < 2x - 5 \leq 8$ *This is like solving 2 inequalities at the same time.*
$\quad 8 < 2x \leq 13$ *First add 5 to each part.*
$\quad 4 < x \leq 6.5$ *Then divide throughout by 2.*
The integer solutions are 5 and 6. *Integers are whole numbers.*

Example

Solve $x^2 < 16$ for integer values.

Answer   *It's tempting to take the square root of both sides and*
The values of x must satisfy: *conclude that $x < 4$, but this is not always true.*
$\quad -4 < x < 4$ *e.g. $-5 < 4$ but $(-5)^2 = 25 > 16$.*
and so the solution is given by: *Note that 0 is an integer and so are the negative*
$-3, -2, -1, 0, 1, 2, 3$ *whole numbers.*

Questions

19.1 Scale factors and percentages

1   Find the scale factors that may be used to calculate the result of the following
    percentage changes:
    a) 8% reduction   b) 3% reduction   c) 40% reduction   d) 32% increase
    e) 50% increase   f) 7% increase   g) 4.8% reduction   h) 0.9% reduction
    i) 0.8% increase j) 140% increase k) 94% reduction   l) 350% increase

2   Add VAT at 17.5% to each of these amounts. Round your answers to the
    nearest penny where appropriate.
    a) £76   b) £4568   c) £124.90   d) £89.99
    e) £357.50   f) £20 480

3   Jayne is offered a special discount of 15% on orders placed with her catalogue.
    If any rounding is carried out to the nearest penny, how much would she
    have to pay for items with the following list prices?
    a) £8.99   b) £25.99   c) £19.95   d) £317.99
    e) £499.99   f) £949.98   g) £49.99   h) £109.99

4 Reduce the following amounts by the percentage shown. Give your answers to 3 S.F.
a) 562; 11%   b) 2.79; 5%   c) 63.7; 1.4%   d) 0.57; 25%
e) 6.8; 0.3%   f) 0.08; 4.2%

5 Increase these amounts by the percentage shown, giving your answers to 3 S.F.
a) 0.97; 50%   b) 12.8; 32%   c) 786; 9%   d) 25.6; 0.8%
e) 4.37; 100%   f) 0.671; 750%

19.2 Reversing the process

6 These prices include VAT at 17.5%. What would they have been without VAT?
a) £676.80   b) £56.40   c) £1 153.85

7 Since young Fred started training seriously for the 100 m sprint he has managed to reduce his time by 8%. If he now runs the race in 11.5 seconds, what was his previous time?

8 Customers complained when they realised that a scale factor of 1.75 had been used to include charges for VAT in the following prices. What were the correct prices?
a) £99.75   b) £421.75   c) £910   d) £28.70
e) £52 500   f) £1.05

9 What single scale factor could be used to correct the error described in question 8?

10 When Mr. Brian Spark received an electricity bill for £135.85 he was delighted. The bill was 5% less than his previous bill and yet he had been expecting a 5% increase.
How much did he expect the bill to be?

19.3 Solving inequalities

11 Find the solution to each of these inequalities:
a) $x + 3 < 8$ b) $x - 4 > 2.7$ c) $x + 1.8 < 10$
d) $2x \geq 6.4$ e) $3x < 5.4$ f) $1.7x \leq 17$
g) $x + 7 > 3$ h) $x - 8.5 \leq -2$ i) $x + 3.6 > -2$

12 Solve the following inequalities and illustrate the solutions using a number line:
a) $2x + 3 > x + 11$ b) $3(x - 2) \geq 2x + 4$ c) $9 - (10 - 3x) \leq 11 + x$
d) $\frac{x}{3} < 5$ e) $\frac{x+7}{3} \geq 4$ f) $\frac{x-2}{5} > 2 - x$

13 List the integer values of x that satisfy these inequalities:
a) $4 < 2x < 13$ b) $7 < 3x + 1 \leq 16$ c) $-9 \leq 2x + 3 < 5$
d) $-17 \leq 4x - 1 < 10$ e) $x^2 \leq 25$ f) $x^2 - 7 < 11.4$

TRANSFORMATIONS

Enlargements

In each diagram the transformation maps figure A onto figure B.

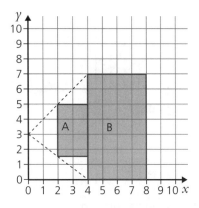

This is an enlargement with scale factor 2 and the centre of enlargement at $(0, 3)$. The lengths of the sides of figure B are all twice as long as those of figure A. The distance from the centre of enlargement has also doubled. A and B are **similar**.

If (and only if) the centre of enlargement is at the origin $(0, 0)$, the coordinates of the enlarged figure can be found by multiplying the coordinates of the original figure by the scale factor.

Enlargements with a fractional scale factor

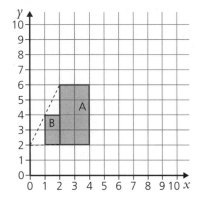

This is an enlargement with scale factor $\frac{1}{2}$ and the centre of enlargement at $(0, 2)$.

The lengths of the sides of figure B are all half as long as those on figure A. The distance from the centre of enlargement is now half of what it was.

Reflections

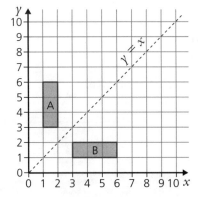

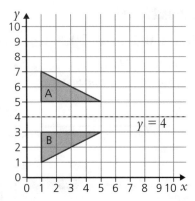

This shows a reflection in the line $y = x$.

This shows a reflection in the line $y = 4$.

Rotations

Rotations are normally described in an *anticlockwise* direction.

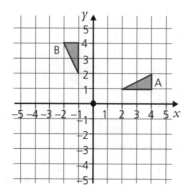 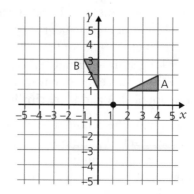

This shows a rotation of 90° about the origin $(0, 0)$.

This shows a rotation of 90° about the point $(1, 0)$.

Translations

This shows a translation of 3 in the x direction and -1 in the y direction.

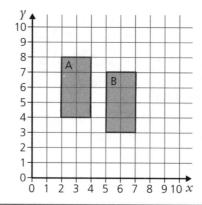

Questions

20.1, 20.2 and 20.3 Enlargements

For questions 1 to 3, copy each diagram. Draw the image of the original figure using an enlargement with the given centre of enlargement and scale factor.

1 Scale factor $\frac{1}{2}$, centre $(5, 5)$

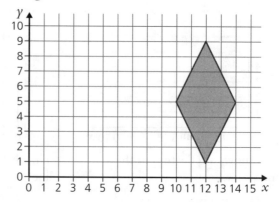

2 Scale factor 3, centre $(3, 0)$

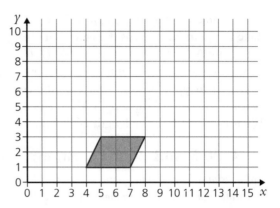

3 Scale factor $\frac{1}{5}$, centre $(0, 0)$

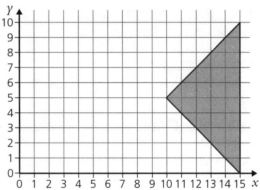

4

a) First enlarge the square using a scale factor of $\frac{1}{2}$, centre $(3, 5)$.

b) Then enlarge the *image* using a scale factor of 4, centre $(7, 5)$.

c) What transformation would map the first square directly onto the third?

5 Draw x and y axes extending from 0 to 10. Take the origin as the centre of enlargement. Draw the triangle A $(1, 3)$, B $(1, 1)$, C $(2, 1)$. Enlarge this triangle with a scale factor of 3. Write down the coordinates of the enlarged triangle A′, B′, C′.
What is the ratio of the length A′B′ : length AB?

6   Draw x and y axes extending from 0 to 12.
Take the point C (2, 1) as the centre of enlargement.
The point A (3, 2) is mapped onto A′ (7, 6).
What is the scale factor of the enlargement? Using the same transformation
B (3, 3) is mapped onto B′. What are the coordinates of B′?
What is the ratio of the length A′B′ : length AB?
What is the ratio of the length B′C′ : length BC?

20.4, 20.5 and 20.6 Rotations, reflections and translations

For questions 7 to 9 draw x and y axes which extend from −10 to +10.
Each question starts with triangle ABC which has A (1, 1), B (4, 2) and C (3, 6).

7   Rotate triangle ABC 90° anticlockwise about the origin. What are the
coordinates of its image $A_1B_1C_1$?
Now reflect the triangle $A_1B_1C_1$ about the x-axis. What are the coordinates of
the second image $A_2B_2C_2$?
Which single transformation will map triangle ABC straight onto triangle
$A_2B_2C_2$?

8   Reflect triangle ABC about the y-axis and write down the coordinates of its
image, $A_1B_1C_1$.
Now rotate triangle $A_1B_1C_1$ about the origin through 180°. What are the
coordinates of the new image $A_2B_2C_2$? Which transformation can be used to
map triangle ABC straight onto $A_2B_2C_2$?

9   Translate triangle ABC to triangle $A_1B_1C_1$ by moving each point 2 units in
the x direction and −3 units in the y direction. Write down the coordinates
of $A_1B_1C_1$.
Next transform triangle $A_1B_1C_1$ to
triangle $A_2B_2C_2$ by translating each
point −7 units in the x direction and 4
units in the y direction. Give the
coordinates for $A_2B_2C_2$. Which
transformation will map triangle ABC
directly onto $A_2B_2C_2$?

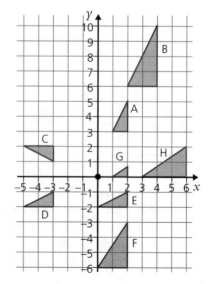

10   Which transformation will map:
a) A onto B   b) A onto C
c) C onto D   d) A onto D
e) D onto E   f) F onto H
g) H onto G ?

SIMULTANEOUS EQUATIONS

This diagram shows the graphs of the equations $y = x + 3$ and $x + y = 7$. The point at which the graphs intersect is of particular interest since it gives us information about *both* equations.

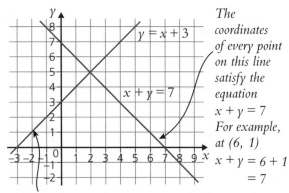

The coordinates of every point on this line satisfy the equation $x + y = 7$ For example, at (6, 1) $x + y = 6 + 1$ $= 7$

The coordinates of the point where the lines intersect must satisfy both equations at the same time, i.e. simultaneously, since the point lies on both lines.

The coordinates of every point on this line satisfy the equation $y = x + 3$
For example, at (–2, 1) $x + 3 = –2 + 3 = 1 = y$

(*Check*: at (2, 5) $x + 3 = 2 + 3 = 5 = y$ and $x + y = 2 + 5 = 7$.)
The simultaneous solution of the equations is therefore given by $x = 2$ and $y = 5$.

An alternative approach to solving simultaneous equations is to use algebra. The idea is to combine the information from both equations in such a way that we are left with a single equation with only one unknown value.

The elimination method

The **coefficient** of a letter in an expression is the number it is multiplied by. For example, in the expression $5x - 7y$, the coefficient of x is 5 and the coefficient of y is -7.

Using the elimination method we *subtract* one equation from the other to eliminate terms that have the *same coefficients*.

Example

Solve the simultaneous equations $x + 3y = 13$ and $x + y = 7$.

Answer
$x + 3y = 13$ (1)   *It's a good idea to label the equations.*
$x + y = 7$ (2)

(1) − (2) gives:
$\qquad 2y = 6$ *The coefficient of x is the same in both equations and so we*
Therefore $y = 3$.   *subtract one equation from the other to eliminate x.*

Substituting for y in (2) gives:
$\qquad x + 3 = 7$ *Once the value of a letter is found, we use this information*
Therefore $x = 4$.   *to find the value of the other letter.*

(*Check*: substituting for x and y in (1) gives: *We should always check that the values*
$x + 3y = 4 + 3 \times 3 = 13$.)   *found make both equations work.*

The solution is $x = 4$, $y = 3$.

To eliminate terms which have *opposite signs* the equations must be *added*.

Example

Solve the equations $7x - 6y = 29$ and $2x + 3y = 13$.

Answer

$7x - 6y = 29$ $\quad$ (1)	*As it stands, the coefficients in the two equations*
$2x + 3y = 13$ $\quad$ (2)	*don't match, but if both sides of equation (2) are*
	multiplied by 2 then y may be eliminated.

Equation (2) $\times$ 2 gives:

$4x + 6y = 26$ $\quad$ (3)

Equation (1) + equation (3) gives:

$\quad 11x = 55$

$\quad\quad x = 5$ $\quad\quad\quad$ *To find y we substitute into the simplest equation.*

Substituting for x in equation (2) gives:

$\quad 10 + 3y = 13$

$\quad\quad 3y = 3$

$\quad\quad y = 1$

(*Check*: substituting for x and y in (1) gives $7x - 6y = 35 - 6 = 29$.)

The required solution is $x = 5$ and $y = 1$.

Questions

21.1 The graphical approach

1   For each of the points of intersection of the graphs shown below, write a pair of simultaneous equations and state their solution. Check by substitution.

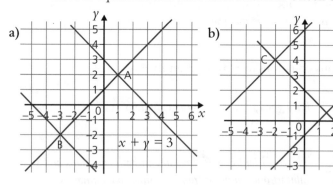

2   Use the diagrams opposite to find the solutions to these simultaneous equations. In each case check your answers by substitution and show your working.

a) $y = x + 1$ b) $y = x - 3$ c) $x + y = 3$ d) $y = x + 3$
    $x + y = 7$ $2y - x = 4$ $y = 2x + 12$ $x - 3y = 1$

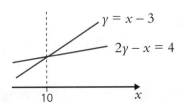

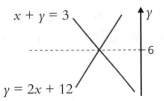

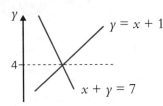

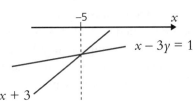

3 Using axes labelled from −5 to 5, draw graphs to solve these equations:

a) $x + y = 5$
   $y = x - 1$

b) $x + 2y = 4$
   $y = x + 5$

c) $4x + y = 0$
   $y = x - 5$

d) $2x + 2y = -9$
   $y = x - 0.5$

21.2 The elimination method

4 Solve these using the elimination method:

a) $5x + 3y = 36$
   $2x + 3y = 18$

b) $x + 7y = 16$
   $2x + 7y = 19$

c) $2v + 5t = 4$
   $v + 5t = 12$

d) $2e - 4n = 2$
   $e + 4n = 31$

e) $2a + 4b = 52$
   $7a - 4b = 2$

f) $4g - 5h = 5$
   $3g - 5h = -5$

g) $4s - 3t = 12$
   $s - t = 1$

h) $5p - 3q = 15$
   $2p + q = 50$

21.3 Solving problems

5 The letters x and y represent the same values in both of the diagrams below.

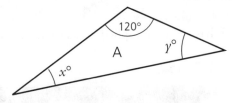

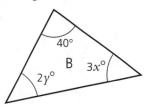

Form two equations in x and y. Solve the equations and use the answers to find the sizes of the unknown angles in each triangle.

6 Use the diagram to form a pair of simultaneous equations in p and q.
Solve the equations and express the ratio $p:q$ in its simplest form.

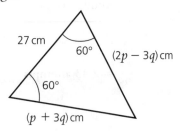

FREQUENCY TABLES

Finding the median from a frequency table

The median is the middle value in a set of results. Data which have been organised onto a frequency table are arranged in order, so it is possible to find the median directly from the table.

To do this, we must find the **cumulative frequencies** (a running total of the frequencies). Here is a frequency table showing the number of times a sample of 28 people had to take their driving test before they passed:

Number of attempts needed	Frequency f	Cumulative frequency
1	12	12
2	8 $\quad$ 8 + 12 = 20	20
3	3 $\quad$ 3 + 20 = 23	23
4	2	25
5	2	27
9	1	28

As there are 28 people (an even number of results) the median is midway between the 14th and 15th results. These both come in the category '2 attempts' so the median number of attempts is 2.

The 14th and 15th results must be in this group

Finding the mean from a frequency table

The mean = $\dfrac{\text{total of all the results}}{\text{number of results}}$

For a straightforward list of numbers:

$\bar{x} = \dfrac{\sum x}{n}$ where $\bar{x}$ = mean

$\sum x$ = total of results

n = number of results

For a frequency table each result has to be multiplied by its frequency f so:

$\bar{x} = \dfrac{\sum fx}{\sum f}$

Here again are the data from the driving test survey:

$\bar{x} = \dfrac{\text{total number of attempts}}{\text{number of people}}$

$= \dfrac{\sum fx}{\sum f}$

$= \dfrac{68}{28} = 2.43$ attempts

Number of attempts x	Frequency f	Attempts × frequency $x \times f$
1	12	1 × 12 = 12
2	8	2 × 8 = 16
3	3	3 × 3 = 9
4	2	4 × 3 = 12
5	2	5 × 2 = 10
9	1	9 × 1 = 9
	TOTAL 28	TOTAL 68

Finding the mean from a grouped frequency table

Continuous data are usually presented in a *grouped* frequency table. Discrete data which cover a wide range may also have to be grouped. We no longer know the exact value for any of the results. The middle value in each class interval (or group) is taken as the value of '*x*'.

The mean is found by:

$$\bar{x} = \frac{\sum fx}{\sum f}$$

(where x is the middle of each class interval)

Example

Find the mean pulse rate from these data:

Pulse rates counted in beats per minute			
Number of beats x	Frequency f	Middle of class interval x	Middle × frequency $x \times f$
60–64	1	62	62
65–69	3	67	201
70–74	6	72	432
75–79	11	77	847
80–84	5	82	410
85–89	2	87	174
90–94	2	92	184
	TOTAL 30		TOTAL 2310

Answer

Here the mean, $\bar{x} = \dfrac{\text{total for } x \times f}{\text{total for } f} = \dfrac{\sum fx}{\sum f}$

$\bar{x} = \dfrac{2310}{30} = 77$ beats per minute

Using a scientific calculator to find the mean

Most scientific calculators have statistical functions programmed into them. Look for these symbols on your calculator:

$\bar{x}$ mean
$\sum x$ total of results
n number of results
Note: $\bar{x} = \dfrac{\sum x}{n}$

These symbols are usually the *second function* for a button and to use them you will need to find the second function button on your calculator. Look in the top left-hand corner for

SHIFT   or   INV   or   2nd fn

22 Frequency tables

Next you need to access these statistical functions by putting your calculator into *statistics mode*. This is shown as SD or STAT on the display. Some calculators have a MODE button and a list of modes under the display.

The following procedure is for scientific calculators. Programmable calculators and graphics calculators may work differently. Please refer to your calculator manual.

To find the mean of a list of numbers:

Step 1 Get your calculator into statistics mode.

Step 2 Clear the statistics memory:

Press $\begin{cases} \text{SHIFT} \\ \text{or} \quad \boxed{\text{INV}} \quad \text{(whichever you have top left)} \\ \text{or} \quad \boxed{\text{2nd fn}} \end{cases}$

then press $\boxed{\text{AC}}$ (usually a red button)

Step 3 Enter the data (for example, the numbers 1, 2 and 3):

e.g.   1 $\boxed{\text{M+}}$

2 $\boxed{\text{M+}}$

3 $\boxed{\text{M+}}$

(If you don't have a button labelled $\boxed{\text{M+}}$ look for one labelled $\boxed{\text{DATA}}$ or $\boxed{\text{DT}}$)

Step 4 Obtain the results:

Press $\begin{cases} \text{SHIFT} \\ \text{or} \quad \boxed{\text{INV}} \quad \text{(whichever you have top left)} \\ \text{or} \quad \boxed{\text{2nd fn}} \end{cases}$

then $\boxed{\bar{x}}$ to find the mean

To find the mean of a frequency table:
Use steps 1 and 2 as before.

Step 3 Enter the data.

To enter the data in this table, do this:

x	f
1	14
2	29
3	33
4	24

1 $\boxed{\times}$ 14 $\boxed{\text{M+}}$

2 $\boxed{\times}$ 29 $\boxed{\text{M+}}$

3 $\boxed{\times}$ 33 $\boxed{\text{M+}}$

4 $\boxed{\times}$ 24 $\boxed{\text{M+}}$

(*Note*: do not press = at any time.)

Step 4   Obtain your results as before:

$\boxed{n}$ gives you Σf.

$\boxed{\Sigma x}$ gives you $\Sigma f x$.

Questions

22.1, 22.2 and 22.3 Means and medians

1   Ramesh conducted a survey in which he recorded the number of working days taken for the delivery of first-class and second-class letters.

First-class	
Number of days	Frequency
1	35
2	3
3	2
4	1
7	1

Second-class	
Number of days	Frequency
1	5
2	28
3	18
4	2
5	2
10	1

Find the mode, median and range for both first-class and second-class letters. Discuss the differences between the two sets of results.

2   This table gives the number of people living in each household in the UK in 1961 and 1991:

a) Find the median household size for both years.
b) On the same diagram, draw a bar line graph with both years shown side by side like this:

Household size	Percentage	
	1961	1991
1 person	12	26
2 people	30	34
3 people	23	17
4 people	19	16
5 people	9	6
6 or more people	7	2

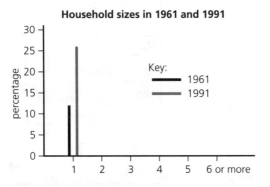

Household sizes in 1961 and 1991

Key:
━━━ 1961
━━━ 1991

c) Write about the changes which took place between 1961 and 1991 in the sizes of households.

3 The number of children in each of 40 families is recorded here:
a) Which column gives the frequency?
b) Find the median number of children per family.

Number of children	Number of families
1	4
2	26
3	6
4	3
5	0
6	1

4 Find the mean for each of the five sets of results in questions 1 to 3.

5 Fifty people who have attended a slimmers' support group lost the following amounts of weight during their diets. Find the mean weight lost.

Weight loss (in kg)	Frequency
$0 \leq w < 2$	2
$2 \leq w < 4$	6
$4 \leq w < 6$	6
$6 \leq w < 8$	14
$8 \leq w < 10$	10
$10 \leq w < 12$	9
$12 \leq w < 14$	3

6 In a school athletics competition, the results for the discus throws were measured and recorded on this frequency table. Find the mean length of throw in metres.

Length (m)	Frequency
$20 \leq x < 25$	10
$25 \leq x < 30$	17
$30 \leq x < 35$	13
$35 \leq x < 40$	13
$40 \leq x < 45$	6
$45 \leq x < 50$	1

7 The weights of 50 male hospital patients are as given in the table. Find their mean weight.

Weight (in kg)	Frequency
60–	2
65–	8
70–	15
75–	21
80–	3
85–90	1

8   30 students were asked to keep a diary to record the number of hours they spent watching TV during that week. Their totals for TV watching times have been summarised on this frequency table. What is the mean number of hours they spent watching TV?

Time	Frequency
$0 \leq t < 10$	7
$10 \leq t < 20$	8
$20 \leq t < 30$	12
$30 \leq t < 40$	2
$40 \leq t < 50$	1

22.4 Calculator means

Use your calculator to find the mean for each list of numbers given below.

9   The sound intensity levels measured in decibels at 12 construction sites were:

     63   59   77   60   57   63
     62   64   73   60   70   71

What is the mean intensity level?

10   The numbers of gulls recorded by an ornithologist on 7 consecutive days were:

     123, 115, 108, 89, 117, 121, 102

What was the mean number of gulls recorded? Give your answer to one decimal place.

11   The lengths of 10 leaves taken from a laurel bush were:

     87 mm   176 mm   102 mm   119 mm   98 mm
     136 mm   129 mm   153 mm   121 mm   138 mm

Find the mean leaf length.

12   The weights of ten 10p coins were:

     11.25 g   10.92 g   11.08 g   11.01 g   11.32 g
     11.37 g   11.23 g   11.18 g   11.21 g   11.22 g

What was the mean weight?

13   To practice finding the mean of data in frequency tables (using your calculator), use the results given in questions 1 to 3.

14   To practice finding the mean of grouped frequency tables (using your calculator), use the data given in questions 5 to 8.

PATTERNS AND PRIMES

Further sequences

If the formula for the nth term of a sequence takes the form $u_n = an + b$, where a and b have fixed values, then the value of a is given by the differences of consecutive terms. Once the value of a is known, the value of b may be calculated using the value of any term.

Example

a) The first four terms of a sequence are 7, 12, 17 and 22. Find a formula for the nth term.

b) The tenth term of a sequence is 49. Find a formula for the nth term if the next two terms are 46 and 43.

Answer

a) The differences have a fixed value of 5 and so $u_n = 5n + b$ for some value of b. The first term is given by $u_1 = 5 \times 1 + b = 7$ and so $b = 2$.

It follows that the formula for the nth term is $u_n = 5n + 2$.

(*Check*: $5 \times 2 + 2 = 12$, $5 \times 3 + 2 = 17$ and $5 \times 4 + 2 = 22$.)

b) The value of the difference is -3 each time and so $u_n = -3n + b$ for some value of b. However this would normally be written as $u_n = b - 3n$.

The tenth term is given by $u_{10} = b - 3 \times 10 = 49$ and so $b = 79$.

The nth term may now be given as $u_n = 79 - 3n$.

(*Check*: $79 - 3 \times 11 = 46$ and $79 - 3 \times 12 = 43$.)

If the formula for the nth term is a *quadratic* then the first differences are not constant but the *second differences* always are. This helps us recognise sequences based on a quadratic rule.

Prime factors

The results of writing numbers as products of their prime factors may be combined to give new information.

Example

Use these results to answer the following questions:
$$360 = 2^3 \times 3^2 \times 5 \qquad 54 = 2 \times 3^3 \qquad 12\,600 = 2^3 \times 3^2 \times 5^2 \times 7$$

■ *What is 3600 as a product of its prime factors?*
$$3600 = 360 \times 10 = (2^3 \times 3^2 \times 5) \times 2 \times 5 = 2^4 \times 3^2 \times 5^2$$

2 may be considered as 2^1 and 5 as 5^1. Powers of the same number are added when we multiply.

■ *How can we recognise that 3600 is a perfect square?*
All of the powers of its prime factors are even. It follows that 3600 may be written as the product of two numbers with identical prime factors, i.e. $3600 = (2^2 \times 3 \times 5) \times (2^2 \times 3 \times 5)$.

■ *What is the smallest whole number that we can multiply 12 600 by to make a perfect square?*
Two of the prime factors of 12 600 are raised to an odd power. If we multiply by 2×7 then all of the powers will be even. It follows that 14 is the required number.

■ *Is 360 divisible by 54?*
No. 54 contains a higher power of 3 than 360.

■ *Is 12 600 divisible by 360?*
Yes. 12 600 contains all of the factors of 360.
(*Note*: $12\,600 \div 360 = (2^3 \times 3^2 \times 5^2 \times 7) \div (2^3 \times 3^2 \times 5) = 5 \times 7 = 35$.)

Questions

23.1 Further sequences

1 The first three terms of a sequence take the form $(4 \times 1) - 2$, $(4 \times 2) - 2$ and $(4 \times 3) - 2$.
   a) Write the next two terms of the sequence in the same way.
   b) Write an expression for the 50th term.
   c) Find a formula for the nth term.
   d) Find the 30th term of the sequence $2, 6, 10, 14, 18, \ldots$
   e) Find the 25th term of the sequence $1, 5, 9, 13, 17, \ldots$

2 Find a formula for the nth term of each of these sequences. In each case, the values shown are the *first* four terms.
   a) $19, 21, 23, 25$
   b) $16, 23, 30, 37$
   c) $9, 15, 21, 27$
   d) $14, 15.5, 17, 18.5$
   e) $10, 10.8, 11.6, 12.4$
   f) $3, 7.7, 12.4, 17.1$
   g) $25, 20, 15, 10$
   h) $16, 10, 4, -2$
   i) $1, -3, -7, -11$
   j) $-10, -12, -14, -16$
   k) $7, 4.6, 2.2, -0.2$
   l) $-5, -6.5, -8, -9.5$

3 The 15th, 16th and 17th terms of a sequence are $68, 72$ and 76.
   a) Find the values of the 14th and the 18th terms.
   b) Find a formula for the nth term.
   c) What is the first term?

4 The first four terms of a sequence are $17, 23, 29$ and 35.
   a) Find a formula for the nth term.
   b) Does the value 157 belong to the sequence? Explain your answer.
   c) Which term of the sequence has the value 263?
   d) How many terms of the sequence are less than 395?

5 The first four terms of a sequence are $175, 164, 153$ and 142.
   a) Find a formula for the nth term.
   b) Which term of the sequence has the value 43?
   c) How many terms are positive?
   d) Which term has the value -89?

6 The first four terms of a sequence are 5, 11, 18 and 26.
   a) Explain why the rule for the nth term cannot be in the form $u_n = an + b$.
   b) Find the second differences.
   c) What do the second differences tell us about the rule for the nth term?
   d) Given that the the nth term is of the form $u_n = n^2 + 3n + c$, find the value of c.
   e) Find the value of the 20th term.
   f) Find the value of the 100th term.

7 The diagrams below follow a pattern.

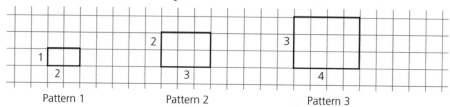

Pattern 1   Pattern 2   Pattern 3

The dimensions of the rectangles may be written as (1 by 2), (2 by 3),(3 by 4), ...
   a) What are the dimensions of the next three rectangles in the pattern?
   b) Find an expression for the dimensions of pattern n.
   c) Calculate the areas of the first five patterns and write them as a sequence (ignore units).
   d) Find the second differences of the sequence found in part c).
   e) Find a formula for the nth term of the sequence and explain the connection with part d).

23.2 Prime factors

8 Copy and complete these factor tree diagrams. Use the results to write 490 and 1400 as products of their prime factors using index notation.

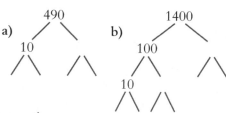

9 Use these results to answer the following questions:
   $450 = 2 \times 3^2 \times 5^2$ $2940 = 2^2 \times 3 \times 5 \times 7^2$ $1750 = 2 \times 5^3 \times 7$
   a) What is 29 400 as a product of its prime factors?
   b) What is 450×1750 as a product of its prime factors?
   b) Is 2940 divisible by 450? Explain how you were able to decide.
   c) What is the smallest whole number that 1750 may be multiplied by so that the result is divisible by 450?
   d) What is the smallest whole number that 2940 should be multiplied by to make a perfect square?
   e) What is the smallest square number that is divisible by 450?
   f) Find the value of $\sqrt[3]{7 \times 450 \times 2940}$ without using a calculator.

10 Express each of the following numbers as the product of its prime factors.
   a) 6650   **b)** 2484   **c)** 25 575   **d)** 29 029   **e)** 31 031   **f)** 101 101

11 Without doing any calculations, write 47 047 as a product of its prime factors. Explain how the method works.

12 Which of the following are prime numbers? Show your method clearly.
   a) 149   **b)** 209   **c)** 211   **d)** 1387

24 AREAS AND VOLUMES

Perimeter

The perimeter of a shape is the distance round the outside.
The perimeter of a circle is called the **circumference**.
The formula for the circumference c is $c = 2\pi r$ or $c = \pi d$; where r is the radius, d is the diameter and the value of π is 3.142 (to 3 D.P.).

Area

The formulae for the areas of various shapes are given here:

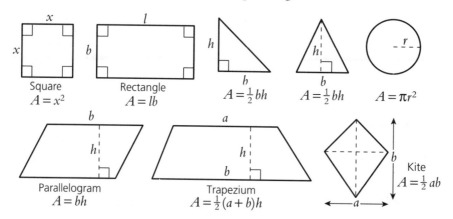

Square
$A = x^2$

Rectangle
$A = lb$

$A = \frac{1}{2}bh$

$A = \frac{1}{2}bh$

$A = \pi r^2$

Parallelogram
$A = bh$

Trapezium
$A = \frac{1}{2}(a+b)h$

Kite
$A = \frac{1}{2}ab$

Large areas such as areas of land may be measured in hectares or square kilometres. These are metric units.

The imperial unit for measuring areas of land is the acre.

1 hectare = 2.5 acres (approximately)

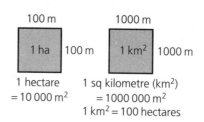

1 hectare
= 10 000 m²

1 sq kilometre (km²)
= 1 000 000 m²
1 km² = 100 hectares

Volumes

A **prism** is any solid which can be cut into slices which are all the same shape (this is called having a uniform cross-section).

Cubes, cuboids and cylinders are all special kinds of prism.

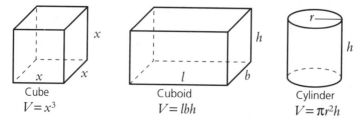

Cube
$V = x^3$

Cuboid
$V = lbh$

Cylinder
$V = \pi r^2 h$

These solids are all examples of prisms.

Volume $V = A \times l$

where A is the area of the cross-section

l is the length

PRISMS

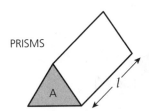 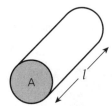 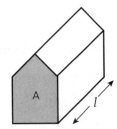

Questions

24.1 and 24.2 Areas of quadrilaterals and circles

1 Find the area of the shaded triangle:

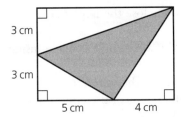

2 a) Find the area of this parallelogram:

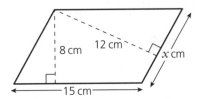

b) Find the value of x.

3 A circular pond of radius 20 metres is surrounded by a path 1 metre wide.

a) Find the area of the pond.

b) Find the area of the path.

c) Find the circumference of the *outside edge* of the path.

4   Find the area of this rhombus if AC is
    15 cm and BD is 12 cm.

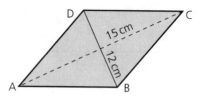

5   The plan, front elevation and side elevation of a shed are drawn below:

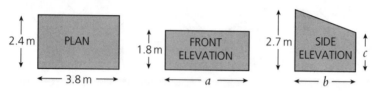

a) What are the measurements of a, b and c?
b) What is the perimeter of the floor of the shed?
c) How tall is the back of the shed?
d) What is the area of the back of the shed?

6   A piece of wire 22 m long is to be bent round to enclose the largest area
    possible.
    a) What is the largest area which can be enclosed if a rectangle is made (using
       a whole number of metres for each side)?
    b) What area can be enclosed if a square is made from the wire?
    d) Will a circle enclose a larger area? First find the radius of the circle, then
       use that answer to find the area. (Use $\pi = \frac{22}{7}$.)

24.3 and 24.4 Volumes of cuboids and prisms

7   a) Draw a net for this solid.
    b) Calculate its volume.
    c) Find its surface area.

8   Find the volume of this prism:

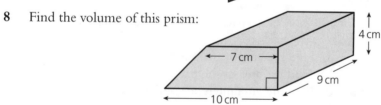

9 The volume of this prism is 720 cm³. What is the height?

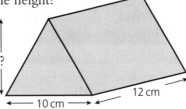

10 cm   12 cm

10 The volume of this prism is 91 cm³.
Find its cross-sectional area A.

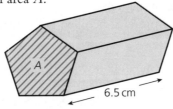

6.5 cm

11 The total surface area of a cube is 54 cm².
a) What is the area of one face?
b) What is the volume of the cube?

12 How many cubic metres of concrete are needed to make a path 30 metres long and 1.3 metres wide if the concrete must be 8 cm deep?

13 A rectangular tank is 5 m long, 2.5 m wide and 1.8 m deep.
a) How many cubic centimetres of water does the tank contain when it is half full?
b) How many litres of water is this?

14 A block of wood 10 cm by 10 cm by 12 cm has a square hole drilled straight through it. The hole measures 8 cm by 8 cm (by 12 cm).
a) Find the volume of wood before the hole is cut.
b) Find the volume of wood remaining after the hole has been cut.

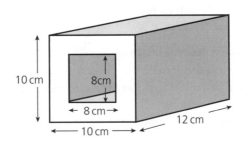

10 cm   8cm   8 cm   12 cm   10 cm

24.5 Volumes of cylinders

15 Find the volume of this gas holder:
a) in m³
b) in litres.

14 m   5 m

16 A large cylindrical drum has a diameter 80 cm and height 120 cm. The drum is filled with oil which is to be poured into smaller containers each holding $1\frac{1}{2}$ litres. How many of these smaller containers can be filled?

17 Six cylindrical tins with radius 6 cm and height 15 cm are to be packed in a box measuring 36 cm by 24 cm by 15 cm tall.
  a) Draw a sketch showing the plan of the box with the tins packed inside it.
  b) What is the volume of the box?
  c) What is the total volume of the 6 tins?
  d) The space in between the tins is to be filled with sawdust. What volume of sawdust is needed?

18 A cylinder with diameter 50 cm contains water to a depth of 70 cm.
  a) What is the volume of the water? (Use $\pi = \frac{22}{7}$.)
  b) The water is to be emptied into a rectangular tank 1.2 m long and 0.8 m wide. Find the area of the base of this tank.
  c) What will be the depth of the water when it is poured into the rectangular tank?

19 A horse trough 2 m long and 60 cm wide is to be filled with water.

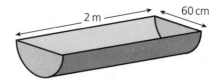

  a) Find the volume of the trough in litres.
  b) If a hose pipe can be used to fill the trough at a steady rate of 8 litres per minute, how long will this take (in minutes)?
  c) If the farmer turns the water on at 7 am, at what time should he come back to turn it off?

20 A circular pond has a radius of 11 m.
  a) Find the area of the surface of the pond.
  b) Last winter the pond froze to a depth of 10 cm. Find the volume of the ice in m³.
  c) Find the weight of the ice if 1 m³ of ice weighs 920 kg.

ALGEBRA AND GRAPHS (2)

Further rearrangements

The advice given earlier in the book when solving equations and inequalities involving x was to try to keep the number of xs positive, i.e. to keep the *coefficient* of x positive. However, an awareness of alternative methods not only provides us with a choice but may also contribute to our understanding.

Example

Solve the inequality $12 - 3x < 7.5$.

Answer

■ Method (i)

$12 - 3x < 7.5$
$12 < 7.5 + 3x$
$4.5 < 3x$
$1.5 < x$
$x > 1.5$

■ Method (ii)

$12 - 3x < 7.5$
$-3x < -4.5$
$x > 1.5$

The final step of method (i) involved writing the statement in the reverse order, so that x appears on the left. It is important that the direction of the inequality symbol is also reversed. Multiplying or dividing an inequality by a negative number will, again, reverse its direction as seen in method (ii).

A type of equation, not so far considered, is where the unknown value appears in the denominator. One technique for solving such equations involves multiplying both sides by the denominator.

Example

Solve these equations:

a) $\dfrac{8}{x} = 0.731$

b) $\dfrac{3.72}{x - 4} = 0.8713$

c) $\dfrac{x + 3}{x - 1} = 4$

Answer

a) $\dfrac{8}{x} = 0.731$

$8 = 0.731x$

$x = \dfrac{8}{0.731}$

$x = 10.9$ (to 3 S.F.)

b) $\dfrac{3.72}{x - 4} = 0.8713$

$3.72 = 0.8713(x - 4)$

$x - 4 = \dfrac{3.72}{0.8713}$

$x = \dfrac{3.72}{0.8713} + 4$

$x = 8.27$ (to 3 S.F.)

c) $\dfrac{x + 3}{x - 1} = 4$

$x + 3 = 4(x - 1)$

$x + 3 = 4x - 4$

$7 = 3x$

$x = \dfrac{7}{3}$

The reciprocal function

The reciprocal of a value x may be written as $\dfrac{1}{x}$ or x^{-1} and means $1 \div x$.

The process of finding the reciprocal may be reversed by finding the reciprocal of the answer, e.g. $2^{-1} = \frac{1}{2}$ and $\left(\frac{1}{2}\right)^{-1} = 2$.

The reciprocal of $\dfrac{a}{b}$ is $\dfrac{b}{a}$.

To find the reciprocal of a mixed number it must first be written as an improper fraction, e.g. $\left(3\frac{1}{2}\right)^{-1} = \left(\frac{7}{2}\right)^{-1} = \frac{2}{7}$.

25 Algebra and graphs (2)

Many formulae involve the use of reciprocals, for example, $\dfrac{1}{R} = \dfrac{1}{R_1} + \dfrac{1}{R_2}$ used in electrical theory.

Example

Use the equation $\dfrac{1}{R} = \dfrac{1}{R_1} + \dfrac{1}{R_2}$ to find R when $R_1 = 7$ and $R_2 = 12$.

Answer

$\dfrac{1}{R} = \dfrac{1}{7} + \dfrac{1}{12}$

Key 7 $\boxed{x^{-1}}$ $\boxed{+}$ 12 $\boxed{x^{-1}}$ $\boxed{=}$

$\dfrac{1}{R} = 0.226\,190\,476$ *To find R take the reciprocal of both sides*

$R = 4.421\,052\,632$

$R = 4.42$ (to 3 S.F.)

The graph of $y = \dfrac{1}{x}$ is shown here.
The lines $y = x$ and $y = -x$ are lines of symmetry.

The graph also has rotational symmetry of order 2 about $(0, 0)$.

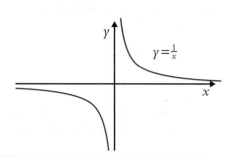

Questions

25.1 Further rearrangements

1 Solve the equation $31 - 5x = 22$ by first:
   a) adding $5x$ to both sides   **b)** subtracting 31 from both sides.

2 Solve the inequality $14 - \dfrac{x}{3} \leq 16$ by first:

   a) adding $\dfrac{x}{3}$ to both sides   **b)** subtracting 14 from both sides.

3 Solve these equations:
   a) $17 - 4u = 9$ **b)** $17 - 4v = 29$ **c)** $42 - 5w = 63 - 8w$

   d) $8 - (p - 5) = 2$ **e)** $24 - (1 - k) = 5k + 9$ **f)** $12 - (t - 5) = 7 + t$

   g) $20 - \dfrac{x}{5} = 19$ **h)** $20 - \dfrac{x}{5} = 21$ **i)** $\dfrac{20 - x}{5} = -1$

   j) $\dfrac{11 - y}{3} = y + 2$ **k)** $\dfrac{f + 1}{4} = 2f - 5$ **l)** $\dfrac{17 - 2g}{3} = g + 1$

4 Solve these inequalities:
   a) $15 - 2y > 9$ **b)** $19 - 3p < 7$ **c)** $21 - 4n < 33$
   d) $6 + 3t \geq 5t$ **e)** $12 + 2h > 6 - 3h$ **f)** $25 + 6k \leq 30 + 8k$

5 Find the value of x to 3 S.F. for each of the following equations:

a) $\dfrac{25}{x} = 1.372$

b) $\dfrac{2.39}{x} = 0.7615$

c) $\dfrac{0.462}{x} = 0.8736$

d) $\dfrac{7}{3x} = 4$

e) $\dfrac{15}{2x} = -11$

f) $\dfrac{9.3}{4x} = 2.7$

6 Solve these equations. In each case, the answer is a whole number.

a) $\dfrac{16}{12-t} = 2$

b) $\dfrac{32}{3n-5} = 2$

c) $\dfrac{12}{1-q} = -2$

d) $\dfrac{2d+3}{d-6} = 5$

e) $\dfrac{h}{h-16} = 3$

f) $\dfrac{x-15}{27-2x} = -\tfrac{1}{3}$

7 a) By considering the gradient of the line AB form an equation involving h.

b) Solve the equation and use the result to find the area of triangle ABC.

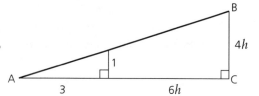

25.2 The reciprocal function

8 a) Copy and complete the table below given that $y = \dfrac{1}{x} + 1$. Round the values of y to 1 D.P. where necessary.

x	−3	−2.5	−2	−1.5	−1	−0.5	−0.25	0.5	1	1.5	2	2.5	3
y			0.5							1.7			

b) Plot the (x, y) values on a graph and join the points with a smooth curve.

c) If the graph were to be extended further to the right, what would happen to the y coordinates of points on the curve?

d) If the graph were to be extended further to the left, what would happen to the y coordinates of points on the curve?

e) Draw two lines of symmetry for the graph and state their equations.

f) Describe any rotational symmetry of the graph.

9 a) Sketch what you think the graph of $y = \dfrac{1}{x} - 1$ should look like.

b) Add any lines of symmetry to your graph and state their equations.

c) Describe any rotational symmetry of the graph.

10 Find the reciprocal of each of these:

a) 7

b) 15

c) $\tfrac{1}{12}$

d) $\tfrac{1}{3}$

e) $\dfrac{p}{q}$

f) $\dfrac{1}{x}$

g) $\dfrac{1}{x+1}$

h) $\dfrac{1}{2x}$

i) $3a - 1$

j) $2\tfrac{1}{2}$

k) $5\tfrac{1}{3}$

l) $3\tfrac{4}{7}$

11 Solve these equations by finding the reciprocal of both sides:

a) $\dfrac{1}{x} = 4$ b) $\dfrac{1}{x} = \dfrac{5}{3}$ c) $\dfrac{1}{x} = -2$ d) $\dfrac{1}{x} = 6\frac{2}{3}$

e) $\dfrac{3}{x} = 6$ f) $\dfrac{9}{x} = 27$ g) $\dfrac{1}{2x} = \dfrac{3}{4}$ h) $\dfrac{1}{x-1} = 4\frac{1}{2}$

12 Use the formula $\dfrac{1}{R} = \dfrac{1}{R_1} + \dfrac{1}{R_2}$ to find the value of R when

$R_1 = 6.8$ and $R_2 = 15.2$.

13 David and James are conducting a survey of vehicles in a car park on three consecutive days. On the first day David works alone and takes 30 minutes to check all the vehicles. The following day James works alone and takes 45 minutes. If there are roughly the same number of vehicles to check each day, how long should they take on the third day if they work together?

PYTHAGORAS AND LOCI

Pythagoras' theorem

Pythagoras' theorem states:

'The square on the hypotenuse of a right-angled triangle equals the sum of the squares on the other two sides.'

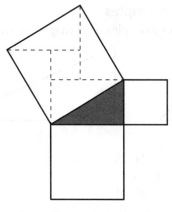

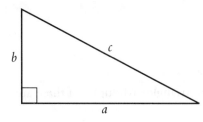

In this right-angled triangle

$$c^2 = a^2 + b^2$$

The hypotenuse is always the longest side in a right-angled triangle and is opposite the right angle.

Using Pythagoras' theorem

Example

Find the length of c.

Answer
Here c is the hypotenuse.

Using $c^2 = a^2 + b^2$:
$$c^2 = 5^2 + 9^2 = 25 + 81 = 106$$
$$c = \sqrt{106}$$
$$c = 10.3 \text{ cm (correct to 1 decimal place)}$$

Example

Find the length of b.

Answer
Here b is *not* the hypotenuse (so is *not* the longest side).

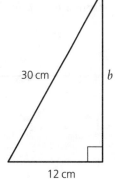

Using $c^2 = a^2 + b^2$:
$$30^2 = 12^2 + b^2$$
$$900 = 144 + b^2$$
$$900 - 144 = b^2$$
$$\sqrt{756} = b$$
$$b = 27.5 \text{ cm (correct to 1 decimal place)}$$

Pythagorean triples

Here are two examples of Pythagorean triples:

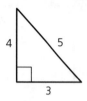 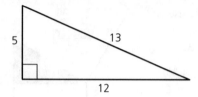

Others are   7, 24, 25
               8, 15, 17
               9, 40, 41

All these 'triples' give the sides of right-angled triangles. Multiples of these are also right-angled triangles.

So from the '3, 4, 5' triple we get:

        6, 8, 10
        $1\frac{1}{2}, 2, 2\frac{1}{2}$
        30, 40, 50, etc.

which are also right-angled triangles (since they are *similar* to the '3, 4, 5' triangle).

Loci

The locus of a point is the set of all the positions it is possible for the point to occupy subject to some given rule or condition. The plural of locus is *loci*.

If an object or point is moving, sketch some of its possible positions to help you decide on its locus.

Examples of loci are as follows:

■ The locus of an object which must move at a *fixed distance* from a *fixed point* (X) is a circle.

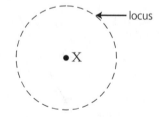

■ The locus of an object which must remain equidistant from *two fixed points* (X and Y) is the *perpendicular bisector* of the line joining X and Y.

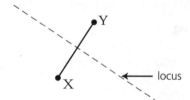

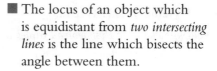

■ An object which must move at a fixed distance from a *line* (of infinite length) has as its locus a pair of parallel lines.

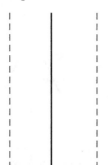

■ The locus of an object which is equidistant from *two intersecting lines* is the line which bisects the angle between them.

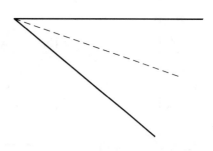

Questions

26.1, 26.2 and 26.3 Pythagoras' theorem

1 a) If angle C = 90°, $a = 3$ and $b = 6$, find c.
   b) If angle C = 90°, $a = 4$ and $c = 8$, find b.
   c) If $a = 7$, $b = 9$ and $c = 12$, is angle C acute, obtuse or 90°?
   d) If $a = 6$, $b = 7$ and $c = 9$, is angle C acute, obtuse or 90°?
   e) If $a = 20$, $b = 21$ and $c = 29$, is angle C acute, obtuse or 90°?

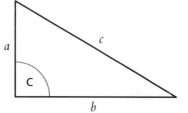

2 A ladder 6.5 m long is leaning against a wall. The bottom of the ladder is 2.5 m away from the wall. How far up the wall does the ladder reach?

3 A rhombus has sides 15 cm long, and one diagonal 18 cm long. Find the length of the other diagonal.

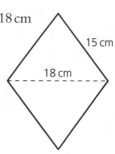

4 Find the lengths of x and y.

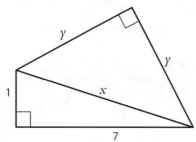

26.4 Pythagorean triples

Use your knowledge of Pythagorean triples to help you solve these problems. (There will be some occasions, however, where you will have to use Pythagoras' theorem.)

5   Find the lengths of the unknown sides:

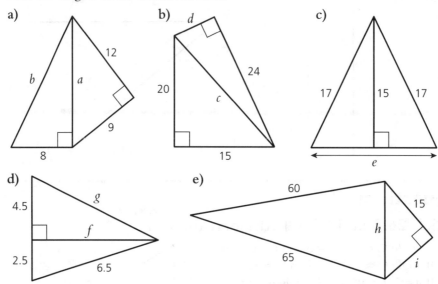

a) 12, b, a, 9, 8
b) d, 24, 20, c, 15
c) 17, 15, 17, e
d) 4.5, g, f, 2.5, 6.5
e) 60, 15, h, 65, i

6   Draw x and y axes extending from 0 to 10.
Plot the points A $(0, 1)$ and B $(8, 7)$.
Find the length of the line joining point A to point B.

7   If A is $(0, 2)$ and B is $(12, 7)$, find the length of AB.

8   Find two whole numbers x and y such that $x^2 + y^2 = 13$. Use your answer to find two even numbers a and b so that $a^2 + b^2 = 52$.

9   Draw a right-angled triangle to construct a line which is $\sqrt{52}$ cm in length.

26.5 and 26.6 Loci

10 If you spin this postcard about CD, what shape is formed by the locus of side AB?

11 This set square is rotated about XY. What shape is formed by the locus of the hypotenuse?

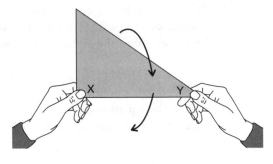

12 This plate is rotated about AB (a diameter of the plate). What shape is formed by the locus of the circumference?

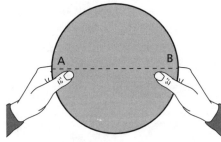

You are advised to use a plastic plate if you try this one out!

13 This concrete post is too heavy to lift, so it is rolled along the ground. The cross section (end) is a square.

a) Sketch the locus of A which is the centre of one end of the block.

b) Sketch the locus of B which is in the centre of one side.

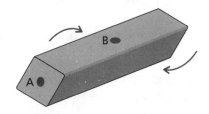

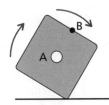

To help you to answer **a)**, cut out a square piece of paper. Make a hole in the centre. Mark the position of the hole as you roll your square along a line.

Can you see how to adapt this idea to help you to answer **b)**?

14 Draw an accurate diagram to show the locus of point P in each case. Show the locus using a dotted line.

a) P is 2 cm from a fixed straight line of indefinite length.

c) P is 3 cm from a straight line XY which is 5 cm long.

c) The line BC is 3 cm long. P is an equal distance from B and C.

d) P is 5 cm from a fixed point A.

27 TRIAL AND IMPROVEMENT

As an alternative to the direct methods of solving equations, considered previously, some equations are most easily solved by substituting an estimate of the solution into the equation and then refining the estimate based on the outcome.

Example

Show that the equation $x^2 + x = 5$ has a solution between 1 and 2 and find the value of this solution correct to two decimal places.

Answer
Make a table like this:

x	$x^2 + x$	
1	2	*too small*
2	6	*too big*
1.5	3.75	*too small*
1.7	4.59	*too small*
1.8	5.04	*too big*

At this stage, the solution is trapped between 1.7 and 1.8 and so the next estimate will include *two* decimal places.

Continuing the process gives:

1.75	4.8125	*too small*
1.78	4.9484	*too small*
1.79	4.9941	*too small*

The solution is now trapped between 1.79 and 1.8 but it isn't yet clear whether the best answer to 2 D.P. is 1.79 or 1.80.

To decide, we try the middle value giving $1.795^2 + 1.795 = 5.017\,025$ which is too big.

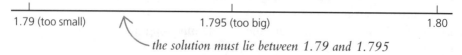

1.79 (too small)   1.795 (too big)   1.80
the solution must lie between 1.79 and 1.795

This shows that the solution is 1.79 to 2 D.P.

Using spreadsheets

Once a spreadsheet is set up to solve a problem it gives the user the power to explore the effect of making changes without having to do the calculations. All of the values shown on the spreadsheet are automatically updated, leaving the user free to consider the impact of the changes made.

Example

Find the positive solution of the equation $x^2 - x = 3$ correct to 1 D.P.

Answer

Spreadsheet

	A	B	C	D	E
1	START	STEP	x	RESULT	
2	2	0.1	2	2	
3			2.1	2.31	
4			2.2	2.64	
5			2.3	2.99	
6			2.4	3.36	
7			2.5	3.75	
8			2.6	4.16	
9					

The spreadsheet above shows that the solution lies between 2.3 and 2.4.

The accuracy may now be improved simply by changing the start value and step size.

Spreadsheet

	A	B	C	D	E
1	START	STEP	x	RESULT	
2	2.3	0.01	2.3	2.99	
3			2.31	3.0261	
4			2.32	3.0624	
5			2.33	3.0989	
6			2.34	3.1356	
7			2.35	3.1725	
8			2.36	3.2096	
9					

The spreadsheet shows that the solution is 2.3 correct to 1 D.P.

Questions

27.1 Solving equations

1   Show that the equation $x^2 - 23 = 0$ has a solution between 4 and 5. Use trial and improvement to find this solution correct to 2 D.P.

2   Copy and complete the process started here to solve the equation $x^3 = 25$ correct to 2 D.P.

x	x^3	
2	8	*too small*
3	27	*too big*
2.5	15.625	

3   One solution of the equation $x^2 - 7x = 4$ is given approximately by $x = 8$. Use trial and improvement to find this solution correct to 2 D.P. Show enough working for your method to be clear.

4   Find the positive solution of each of these equations correct to 3 D.P.

   a) $x^2 + 5x = 31$ b) $x(x - 3) = 15$ c) $x - \dfrac{1}{x} = 1$ d) $x^2 - \dfrac{1}{x} = 2$

27.2 Using spreadsheets

5   The spreadsheet shows the values of $\dfrac{100}{x} - x^2$ for values of x from 1 to 6.

	A	B	C	D	E	
1	START	STEP	x	RESULT		
2	1	1	1	99		
3			2	46		
4			3	24.33333		
5			4	9		
6			5	-5		
7			6	-19.3333		
8						

Spreadsheet

a) The number shown in cell D2 is 99. Show how the formula for this cell must be entered.

b) Between which two whole numbers does the solution of the equation $\dfrac{100}{x} - x^2 = 7$ lie?

6   a) Explain how changing the values for the start and step size can lead to a
      better approximate solution of the equation $\frac{100}{x} - x^2 = 7$.

   b) The information shown below is taken from the spreadsheets used to find
      the value of x to a higher degree of accuracy. In each case state two values
      between which the solution is known to lie.

(i)

C	D
x	RESULT
4	9
4.1	7.580244
4.2	6.169524
4.3	4.765814
4.4	3.367273
4.5	1.972222

(ii)

C	D
x	RESULT
4.1	7.580244
4.11	7.4388
4.12	7.297445
4.13	7.156175
4.14	7.014989
4.15	6.873886

(iii)

C	D
x	RESULT
4.14	7.014989
4.141	7.000875
4.142	6.986762
4.143	6.97265
4.144	6.958538
4.145	6.944427

   c) State the solution of the equation $\frac{100}{x} - x^2 = 7$ to the highest degree of
      accuracy that you can justify based on the above information.

7   This spreadsheet shows values of the expression $20 - x^2 + 9x$ for values of x
    from 4 to 5.

	A	B	C	D	E	
1	START	STEP	x	RESULT		
2	4	0.1	4	40		
3			4.1	40.09		
4			4.2	40.16		
5			4.3	40.21		
6			4.4	40.24		
7			4.5	40.25		
8			4.6	40.24		
9			4.7	40.21		
10			4.8	40.16		
11			4.9	40.09		
12			5	40		
13						

Spreadsheet

Use the symmetry of the results shown to find:
a) the maximum value of the expression $20 - x^2 + 9x$
b) the maximum value of the expression $9x - x^2$.

PREDICTIONS & COMPARISONS

Making predictions

To make predictions from a scatter diagram, use a 'best fit' line like this:

- ■ Draw a straight line through the middle of the points on the graph
- ■ Try to balance stray points above and below the line
- ■ (If you have found the mean, take the 'best fit' line through it)
- ■ Don't try to make predictions too far outside the range of results on the graph (as the situation may change).

Example

How much small shopkeepers have to pay in business rates to the local council depends partly on how far their shop is from the town centre. Here are some data for ten shops of similar size.

Distance (km)	0	0.2	0.5	1.0	1.5	2.2	2.8	2.9	3.5	5.0
Rate (£)	3500	4000	3200	3000	3500	2200	1900	1900	1500	950

Draw a scatter diagram and add the line of best fit. Use it to predict the rates charged to a shop 3 km from the town centre.

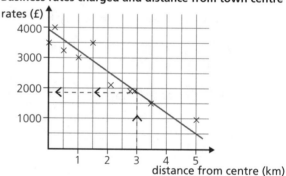

Business rates charged and distance from town centre

Answer
From the scatter diagram, the rates charged to a shop 3 km from the town centre would be £1800.

Making comparisons

Two frequency distributions can be compared by looking at their respective means, medians or modes and their ranges. Another method is to make a visual comparison by drawing super-imposed **frequency polygons**.

Example

This table gives the ages of mothers of all babies born in 1971 and 1991. Draw frequency polygons to show if there is any trend in the data. Do you think there are real differences between mothers' ages in 1971 and 1991, and if so, can you say why?

Live births: by age of mother		
	Percentages	
Age of mother	1971	1991
$15 \le x < 20$	10.6	7.6
$20 \le x < 25$	36.5	24.8
$25 \le x < 30$	31.4	35.6
$30 \le x < 35$	14.1	23.0
$35 \le x < 40$	5.8	7.6
$40 \le x < 45$	1.5	1.2
$45 \le x < 50$	0.1	0.1

Answer

The easiest way to draw a frequency polygon is to join up the midpoints of the tops of the histogram. This diagram shows the frequency polygon plotted in this way for the 1971 mothers.

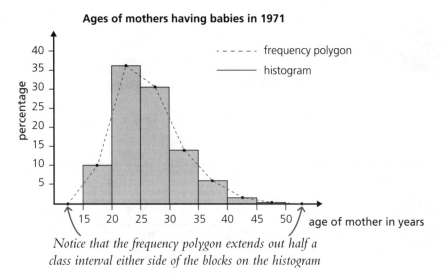

Ages of mothers having babies in 1971

Notice that the frequency polygon extends out half a class interval either side of the blocks on the histogram

Here are the frequency polygons for both years drawn on the same graph:

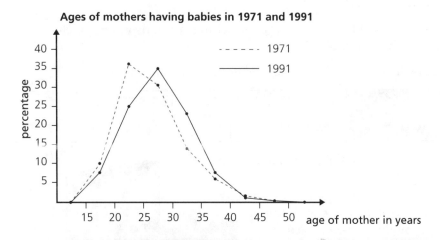

Ages of mothers having babies in 1971 and 1991

The graphs clearly show that there are fewer mothers in the younger age groups (under 25) in 1991 compared to 1971. Instead there are now more mothers aged over 25. The group which has increased most is the 30 to 34 age group. So women seem to be delaying having children, perhaps for career reasons.

Questions

28.1 and 28.2 Making predictions

1 Nigel has done a survey of the fares charged for various bus journeys in his local area. Here are his results:

Distance (km)	1.5	3.0	10.0	4.5	8.0	0.8	0.5	6.2	7.0	2.0
Fare	80p	£1.50	£3.75	£1.70	£3.00	80p	50p	£2.65	£3.00	£1.30

a) Plot a scatter graph showing distance on the horizontal axis.
b) Draw in the line of best fit.
c) If Nigel has to go on a 5 km journey, roughly how much should he expect to pay in fares?

2 This table gives the scores of eight golfers in a competition together with their handicaps.

Handicap	7	12	3	5	12	10	13	18
Score	79	85	76	79	83	82	83	89

a) Plot a scatter graph showing handicap on the horizontal axis.
b) Draw in the line of best fit and predict the score for a golfer with a handicap of 15.

3 Nikki weighed all her school text books, claiming that they were much too heavy to carry round all day!

Here are the weights of each one together with the number of pages:

Number of pages	80	92	100	96	112	128	144	160	160
Weight (g)	168	185	190	205	252	273	305	352	365

a) Plot a scatter graph showing number of pages on the x-axis.
b) Predict the weight of a book with 150 pages using a line of best fit.
c) Can you think of other factors which will affect the weight of the books, besides the number of pages?

28.3 Frequency polygons

4 Jenny has a program on her computer which will measure the time it takes a person to react to a light or to a noise. She decides to investigate any possible differences between the reaction times of adults and children. Here are her results.

   a) Draw frequency polygons for adult and child reaction times on the same graph.
   b) Give the modal class and range for both groups of people.
   c) What does your graph show?

Reaction time (s)	Frequency	
	Adults	Children
$0.14 \leq x < 0.16$	1	2
$0.16 \leq x < 0.18$	2	3
$0.18 \leq x < 0.20$	0	4
$0.20 \leq x < 0.22$	7	7
$0.22 \leq x < 0.24$	22	12
$0.24 \leq x < 0.26$	26	16
$0.26 \leq x < 0.28$	16	20
$0.28 \leq x < 0.30$	13	17
$0.30 \leq x < 0.32$	10	10
$0.32 \leq x < 0.34$	5	8
$0.34 \leq x < 0.36$	0	6
$0.36 \leq x < 0.38$	0	4

5 On a geography field trip Damon's class measured the acidity of the soil on hillsides facing either north or south. (Acidity is measured by the pH value.)

Here are the results:

Soil pH values	Frequency	
	North-facing	South-facing
$3.5 \leq x < 4.0$	0	1
$4.0 \leq x < 4.5$	0	0
$4.5 \leq x < 5.0$	0	3
$5.0 \leq x < 5.5$	1	7
$5.5 \leq x < 6.0$	2	6
$6.0 \leq x < 6.5$	4	1
$6.5 \leq x < 7.0$	7	2
$7.0 \leq x < 7.5$	4	0
$7.5 \leq x < 8.0$	2	0

   a) Draw frequency polygons for north-facing and south-facing slopes on the same diagram.
   b) What does your graph show?
   c) Find the mean pH for north-facing slopes and for south-facing slopes.
   d) Find the modal class and the range for both sets of results.
   e) Which group has the highest mean?
   f) Which group is more variable?

The principle of being able to add and subtract *like terms* has already been established where the terms are algebraic, e.g. $3x + 5x = 8x$ and $7ab - ab = 6ab$. However, expressions such as $3x + 5y$ and $7ab - ac$ involve *unlike* terms and cannot be simplified.

This principle applies equally well when dealing with fractions, e.g.

$\frac{2}{7} + \frac{3}{7}$ may be regarded as $2\left(\frac{1}{7}\right) + 3\left(\frac{1}{7}\right) = 5\left(\frac{1}{7}\right)$

that is, $\qquad \frac{2}{7} + \frac{3}{7} = \frac{5}{7}$

In the same way, $\frac{2}{x} + \frac{3}{x} = \frac{5}{x}$

$\qquad\qquad\qquad \frac{11}{15} - \frac{4}{15} = \frac{7}{15}$

and $\qquad\qquad \frac{11}{x+3} - \frac{4}{x+3} = \frac{7}{x+3}$

We are able to add and subtract fractions that are not expressed in the same terms, i.e. that have different denominators, by using **equivalent fractions**.

Example

Calculate and leave your answers in their simplest terms:

a) $\frac{4}{5} + \frac{7}{10}$ $\qquad$ b) $\frac{5}{8} + \frac{7}{12}$.

Answer

a) $\frac{4}{5} + \frac{7}{10}$ $\qquad$ *$\frac{4}{5}$ is equivalent to $\frac{8}{10}$.*

$\quad = \frac{8}{10} + \frac{7}{10}$ $\qquad$ *The fractions are now expressed in like terms.*

$\quad = \frac{15}{10} = \frac{3}{2}$ $\qquad$ *15 and 10 have a common factor of 5 and so the fraction cancels.*

$\quad = 1\frac{1}{2}$ $\qquad$ *$\frac{3}{2}$ may be written as a mixed number.*

b) $\frac{5}{8} + \frac{7}{12}$ $\qquad$ *24 is a common multiple of 8 and 12. It follows that*

$\quad = \frac{15}{24} + \frac{14}{24}$ $\qquad$ *both fractions may be written with a denominator of 24.*

$\quad = \frac{29}{24} = 1\frac{5}{24}$

Fractions that are expressed in algebraic terms may be added and subtracted in the same way, i.e. by finding equivalent forms that have the same denominator.

Example

Simplify using equivalent fractions:

a) $\frac{3}{x} + \frac{5}{2x}$ $\qquad$ b) $\frac{2}{3} + \frac{1}{x}$

Answer

a) $\frac{3}{x} + \frac{5}{2x}$ $\frac{3}{x}$ is equivalent to $\frac{6}{2x}$.

$= \frac{6}{2x} + \frac{5}{2x}$ Both fractions now have a common denominator of 2x.

$= \frac{11}{2x}$

b) $\frac{2}{3} + \frac{1}{x}$ We can use a common denominator of 3x so now $\frac{2}{3} = \frac{2x}{3x}$ and $\frac{1}{x} = \frac{3}{3x}$.

$= \frac{2x}{3x} + \frac{3}{3x}$

$= \frac{2x+3}{3x}$ Note: this will not simplify further as the numerator and denominator have no common factors.

Whole numbers may also be written as fractions, e.g. $1 = \frac{2}{2} = \frac{7}{7} = \frac{x}{x} = \frac{5y}{5y}$.

This allows us to simplify expressions involving fractions and whole numbers, e.g. $1 - \frac{3}{20} = \frac{20}{20} - \frac{3}{20} = \frac{17}{20}$ and $\frac{3}{x} - 2 = \frac{3}{x} - \frac{2}{1} = \frac{3}{x} - \frac{2x}{x} = \frac{3-2x}{x}$.

Addition and subtraction involving mixed numbers may be carried out by dealing with the whole numbers and fractions separately.

Example

Calculate the value of the following:

a) $2\frac{1}{3} + 5\frac{1}{2}$ **b)** $11\frac{4}{5} - 2\frac{1}{2}$ **c)** $4\frac{5}{8} + 2\frac{3}{4}$ **d)** $10\frac{1}{4} - 4\frac{2}{3}$

Answer

a) $2\frac{1}{3} + 5\frac{1}{2} = 7 + \frac{2}{6} + \frac{3}{6} = 7\frac{5}{6}$

b) $11\frac{4}{5} - 2\frac{1}{2} = 9 + \frac{8}{10} - \frac{5}{10} = 9\frac{3}{10}$

c) $4\frac{5}{8} + 2\frac{3}{4} = 6 + \frac{5}{8} + \frac{6}{8} = 6 + \frac{11}{8} = 6 + 1\frac{3}{8} = 7\frac{3}{8}$

d) $10\frac{1}{4} - 4\frac{2}{3} = 6 + \frac{3}{12} - \frac{8}{12} = 6 - \frac{5}{12} = 5\frac{7}{12}$

Multiplication involving mixed numbers may be done either by treating the fractions separately or by converting to improper fractions. In any given situation, one approach may prove to be easier than the other. *Note:* to divide by a number we **multiply** by its **reciprocal**.

Example

Calculate the value of these expressions:

a) $2\frac{1}{3} \times 5$ **b)** $6\frac{1}{4} \times \frac{3}{5}$ **c)** $5\frac{1}{4} \div 3\frac{1}{2}$

Answer

a) $2\frac{1}{3} \times 5 = \left(2 \times 5\right) + \left(\frac{1}{3} \times 5\right) = 10 + \frac{5}{3} = 10 + 1\frac{2}{3} = 11\frac{2}{3}$

b) $6\frac{1}{4} \times \frac{3}{5} = \frac{25}{4} \times \frac{3}{5} = \frac{15}{4} = 3\frac{3}{4}$

c) $5\frac{1}{4} \div 3\frac{1}{2} = \frac{21}{4} \div \frac{7}{2} = \frac{21}{4} \times \frac{2}{7} = \frac{3}{2} = 1\frac{1}{2}$ (Note: $\frac{2}{7}$ is the reciprocal of $\frac{7}{2}$.)

Questions

29.1 Further fractions

1   Simplify the following:

a) $\frac{2}{9} + \frac{5}{9}$

b) $\frac{11}{15} - \frac{3}{15}$

c) $\frac{9}{17} + \frac{2}{17} + \frac{3}{17}$

d) $\frac{6}{11} - \frac{4}{11} + \frac{1}{11}$

e) $\frac{11}{12} - \frac{5}{12}$

f) $\frac{10}{21} + \frac{4}{21}$

g) $\frac{5}{x} + \frac{3}{x}$

h) $\frac{9}{y} - \frac{7}{y}$

i) $\frac{4}{ab} + \frac{3}{ab} - \frac{5}{ab}$

2   Use equivalent fractions to simplify these:

a) $\frac{2}{5} + \frac{3}{10}$

b) $\frac{1}{4} + \frac{5}{12}$

c) $\frac{7}{8} + \frac{3}{4}$

d) $\frac{7}{12} - \frac{3}{8}$

e) $\frac{8}{9} + \frac{5}{6}$

f) $\frac{5}{12} - \frac{4}{15}$

g) $\frac{5}{x} - \frac{1}{2x}$

h) $\frac{7}{y} - \frac{2}{3y}$

i) $\frac{5}{3a} + \frac{1}{a}$

3   Simplify the following:

a) $1 - \frac{1}{9}$

b) $1 - \frac{5}{12}$

c) $1 - \frac{3}{8}$

d) $5 - \frac{2}{7}$

e) $9 - \frac{4}{5}$

f) $8 - 3\frac{1}{10}$

g) $1 + \frac{5}{x}$

h) $\frac{3}{y} + 2$

i) $\frac{2}{x+3} + 4$

j) $\frac{11}{x} - 1$

k) $\frac{3}{n+1} - 2$

l) $\frac{4}{w-5} - 3$

4   Calculate the value of these:

a) $2\frac{1}{4} + 5\frac{3}{8}$

b) $6\frac{5}{9} + 1\frac{2}{3}$

c) $7\frac{11}{12} - 4\frac{1}{2}$

d) $4\frac{1}{5} - \frac{1}{2}$

e) $8\frac{2}{3} - 5\frac{3}{4}$

f) $2\frac{3}{4} + 3\frac{7}{8} - 1\frac{1}{2}$

g) $3\frac{1}{3} \times 3$

h) $2\frac{1}{2} \times 7$

i) $1\frac{3}{4} \times 4$

j) $6\frac{1}{4} \div 5$

k) $5\frac{1}{2} \div 3\frac{2}{3}$

l) $8\frac{3}{4} \div 4\frac{2}{3}$

5   Copy and complete these statements using fractions:

a) $6 \div ? = 24$

b) $12 \times ? = 2$

c) $20 \times ? = 15$

d) $18 \div ? = 27$

e) $10 \times ? = 25$

f) $16 \div ? = 24$

6   How many glasses may be filled from a 3-litre bottle of lemonade if each glass holds $\frac{1}{6}$ litre?

7 James earns £4.50 per hour at the standard rate but overtime is paid at time-and-a-half. How much does James earn for each hour of overtime?

8 When a company's profits were announced they showed an increase of $\frac{1}{3}$, based on last year's performance.
a) If the profit last year was £$7\frac{1}{2}$ million, what is the profit for this year?
b) What scale factor could be used to calculate this year's profit from last year's?
c) If the figure for this year is £14 million, what was the profit last year?

9 One fifth of the pupils in a year 11 group wear glasses and two out of three of these are girls.
a) What fraction of the group do not wear glasses?
b) What fraction of the group is made up of girls who wear glasses?
c) If there are 30 pupils in the group, how many are boys who wear glasses?

10 Exactly $\frac{1}{8}$ of the seeds that I sowed failed to germinate. Of the remaining seeds exactly $\frac{3}{4}$ produced plants of the colour that I wanted.
a) What is the smallest number of seeds that I could have sowed?
b) Use your answer to part **a)** to find the number of plants I obtained of the right colour.

USING PROBABILITY

The relative frequency of an event is found by:

> Relative frequency = $\dfrac{\text{number of times that event occurred}}{\text{total number of trials}}$

The relative frequency of an event tells us what proportion of the time we can expect that event to happen. It is a very useful way of estimating probabilities in real-life situations where the outcomes are not equally likely.

For example, Joel conducted an experiment to find the relative frequency of a drawing pin landing either point upwards or on its side like this:

He put 10 drawing pins in a cup, then shook them out onto the table. He counted the numbers landing in each position, then repeated the procedure 9 more times. Out of 100 drawing pins, he found that 28 landed point up.

The relative frequency of a drawing pin landing point up was $\frac{28}{100}$ or 0.28.

The relative frequency of a drawing pin landing on its side was $\frac{72}{100}$ or 0.72.

Questions

30.1, 30.3 and 30.4 Finding relative frequencies

Choose one of the three experiments described here.

1 Collect 200 single-figure random numbers. Record your results carefully so that you can calculate the required relative frequencies.

You may either:
 (i) generate random numbers on your calculator, or
 (ii) use the last figure in each phone number on a page chosen at random from your local directory.

Random numbers using a calculator
To generate random numbers your calculator will have a button labelled Ran# .
(If your calculator does not have this button, refer to its instructions.)

If you press Ran# you will see something like this on your display:

   0.371

Strictly speaking the Ran# key produces a random number, usually to 3 D.P., and lying between 0 and 1. However for *this* simulation, ignore the 0 and decimal point at the front, and take 3, 7 and 1 as three random numbers. Each time you press Ran# you will get three new random numbers.

Whichever method of obtaining random numbers you choose:

a) Before you begin, estimate how many of each number, 0 to 9, you expect to get.

b) Record your results on a tally chart.

c) Count up the frequencies at the end.

d) Find the relative frequency for an even number (remember 0 is an even number!).

e) Are your results much different from those you expected to get?

2   Place two coins in a plastic cup.

Shake them out onto the table. Count the number of heads and record your results on a tally table. Record your results carefully so that you can calculate the required relative frequencies.

Number of heads	Tally	Frequency
0		
1		
2		
	Total	60

a) Before you start, try to estimate how many results you expect to get for each of the outcomes 0, 1 or 2 (assuming you are to repeat the experiment 60 times).

b) Find the relative frequency for each outcome.

c) Which outcome seems to be most likely to occur?

d) Is this result surprising?

3   Shuffle a pack of cards and pick out three cards.

Is there a heart among the three cards you have chosen? Record your results on a tally chart like this:

Outcome	Tally	Frequency
At least one heart		
No hearts		
	Total	100

Record your results carefully so that you can calculate the required relative frequencies.

a) Before you begin, try to estimate how many times you will find at least one heart (if you are to repeat the experiment 100 times.)

b) Calculate the relative frequency of obtaining at least one heart.

30.2 Cracking a code

4   The following passage has been written in code. Can you decipher it?

You will need the result of your 'Top ten letters' found during your work in class.

The code used for this passage, however, is different from the code used for the passage in the Classbook.

XH UY, HK GHX XH UY
XZJX OP XZY ERYPXOHG
BZYXZYK XOP GHUYK OG XZY
IOGT XH PRSSYK XZY PLOGCP JGT
JKKHBP HS HRXKJCYHRP SHKXRGY
HK XH XJDY JKIP JCJOGPX J PYJ
HS XKHRULYP
JGT UQ HMMHPOGC YGT XZYI?
XH TOY XH PLYYM
GH IHKY JGT UQ J PLYYM XH
PJQ BY YGT XZY ZYJKX-JKZY
JGT XZY XZHRPJGT GJXRKJL
PZHFDP XZY SLYPZ OP ZYOK
XH.

A CHANGE OF FORM

Expressing change as a percentage

The scale factor method for calculating the result of a percentage change (Unit 19) may be adapted to express any given change as a percentage of the original amount.

Example

Before her pay increase, Emma earned £712.51 per month. She now earns £743.67 per month. Express her salary increase in percentage terms.

Answer

Scale factor $= \dfrac{\text{new salary}}{\text{original salary}} = \dfrac{743.67}{712.51} = 1.0437\ldots$ *This means that Emma's new salary is 104.37...% of her original salary.*

So her salary increase as a percentage increase is 4.37% (to 3 S.F.).

Example

Average house prices in the UK fell from a peak of £70 602 in July 1989 to £61 583 in July 1995. Calculate the percentage fall in house prices over this time correct to 1 D.P.

Answer

Scale factor $= \dfrac{61\,583}{70\,602} = 0.872\,255\,7\ldots$ *i.e. the 1995 figure is 87.2% of the 1989 figure*

So the percentage fall is given by $(100 - 87.2)\% = 12.8\%$ correct to 1 D.P.

Alternatively, subtracting 1 from the scale factor gives $-0.127\,744\ldots$, which again may be interpreted as a 12.8% fall correct to 1 D.P.

The **reciprocal** of the scale factor representing a percentage change may be used to express the reverse process as a percentage, e.g. an increase of 14% would be represented by a scale factor of 1.14 and so the scale factor needed to undo this effect is 1.14^{-1} (i.e. $\frac{1}{1.14}$) $= 0.877\,19\ldots$ which corresponds to a reduction of 12.3% to 3 S.F.

Powers and roots

Rules	Examples	
$a^n = \underbrace{a \times a \times a \times \ldots}_{n \text{ terms}}$	$3^4 = 3 \times 3 \times 3 \times 3$	(*Note:* $3^4 = 81 \neq 3 \times 4$)
$a^m \times a^n = a^{m+n}$	$x^3 \times x^5 = x^8$	and $x^{-1} \times x^7 = x^6$
$a^m \div a^n = a^{m-n}$	$x^{12} \div x^3 = x^9$	and $\dfrac{x^4}{x^5} = x^{-1} = \dfrac{1}{x}$
$(a^m)^n = a^{mn}$	$(x^2)^3 = x^6$	and $(x^{-1})^{-1} = x^1 = x$
$a^{-n} = \dfrac{1}{a^n}$	$x^{-2} = \dfrac{1}{x^2}$	and $2^{-3} = \dfrac{1}{2^3} = \dfrac{1}{8}$

Some special results are:

$a^1 = a$ for any value of a,

$a^0 = 1$ provided $a \neq 0$.

Standard form (without a calculator)

Very large and very small numbers are most easily expressed in **standard form** as $A \times 10^n$ where $1 \le A < 10$ and n is an integer, i.e. a positive or negative whole number. For very large numbers n is positive and for very small numbers n is negative.

Example

Write these numbers in standard form:
a) 42 000   **b)** 0.000 000 06   **c)** 0.000 074

Answer
a) 42 000 is written as 4.2×10^4. ←——— *The value of **n** may be thought of as the number of places that the decimal point must be moved to the **right** to restore the place value of the original number.*

A decimal point is needed to ensure that $1 \le A < 10$.

b) 0.000 000 06 is written as 6×10^{-8}.   *Note: $10^{-8} = \dfrac{1}{10^8}$, i.e. 10^{-8} is the reciprocal of 10^8. It follows that multiplying by 10^{-8} has the same effect as dividing by 10^8, which reduces the place value of the 6 to its value in 0.000 000 06.*

c) 0.000 074 is written as 7.4×10^{-5}. ←——— *Interpret this as meaning that the decimal point in 7.4 would be written 5 places further to the **left** in the usual notation.*

Example

Find the value of these in standard form:
a) 34 000 000 × 2 000 000   **b)** 7 000 000 000 × 50 000 000

Answer
a) 34 000 000 × 2 000 000
$= (3.4 \times 10^7) \times (2 \times 10^6)$
$= 6.8 \times 10^{13}$

b) 7 000 000 000 × 50 000 000
$= (7 \times 10^9) \times (5 \times 10^7)$
$= 35 \times 10^{16}$ ←——— *This is not yet in standard*
$= 3.5 \times 10^{17}$ *form because $A > 10$.*

Example

Find the value of these in standard form:
a) $(3.7 \times 10^8) + (6.5 \times 10^8)$
b) $(1.2 \times 10^{15}) - (8.6 \times 10^{14})$
c) $(8.4 \times 10^7) \div (4 \times 10^{-5})$

Answer

a) $(3.7 \times 10^8) + (6.5 \times 10^8) = 10.2 \times 10^8 = 1.02 \times 10^9$ $\leftarrow A > 10$

*Both numbers have the same value of **n**,
and so the place values correspond, allowing
us to add the 3.7 and 6.5 directly.*

b) $(1.2 \times 10^{15}) - (8.6 \times 10^{14}) = (12 \times 10^{14}) - (8.6 \times 10^{14}) = 3.4 \times 10^{14}$

*Writing the first number in this way gives
both numbers the same value of **n**.*

c) $(8.4 \times 10^7) \div (4 \times 10^{-5}) = \dfrac{8.4 \times 10^7}{4 \times 10^{-5}}$

$$= \frac{8.4}{4} \times \frac{10^7}{10^{-5}}$$

$$= 2.1 \times 10^{12} \quad \longleftarrow \textit{Note: } 7 - -5 = 12$$

*Division by 4×10^{-5} has
had an enlarging effect.*

Questions

31.1 Change as a percentage

1 For each of the following pairs of numbers, express the increase from the first to the second as a percentage correct to 3 S.F.
a) 246, 273   b) 715, 826   c) 91.7, 123.8   d) 6.347, 9.126
e) 18.45, 19.37   f) 12.62, 21.73   g) 3.42, 7.83   h) 247.9, 846.3

2 Between 1800 and 1900 the population of the world increased from 954 million to 1633 million.
a) Express this increase as a percentage correct to 2 S.F.
b) Use your answer to part a) to estimate the projected percentage increase from 1900 to the year 2050. Show your working and state any assumptions that you make.
c) One estimate of the population in 2050 based on current trends is 10 000 million. Use this figure to calculate the projected percentage increase from 1900 and comment on how it compares with your own estimate.

3 Calculate the percentage reduction from the first figure to the second in each of these pairs. Give your answers to an accuracy of 3 S.F.
a) 96.4, 78.9   b) 476.3, 475.2   c) 106.8, 65.9   d) 812.7, 372.4
e) 5.67, 1.43   f) 12.62, 1.39   g) 768.3, 764.2   h) 49.62, 49.56

4   During the summer of 1995 water restrictions came into force, due to concern about the low levels of water held in reservoirs around the country, following a prolonged dry spell. Enquiries at the Haweswater reservoir revealed that stocks were down to 25 460 megalitres compared with a normal figure of 42 450 megalitres.
   a) By what percentage were the figures lower than normal?
   b) Given that the capacity of the reservoir is 84 859 megalitres, by what percentage were the stocks below capacity?

5   The price of a computer including VAT at 17.5% is £1 163.25.
   a) What was the price before VAT was added?
   b) By what percentage must £1 163.25 be reduced to obtain the answer given in **a)**?

31.2 Powers and roots

6   Simplify the following expressions:
   a) $z \times z \times z \times z \times z$ **b)** $t^5 \times t^4$ **c)** $j^2 \times j^3 \times j^6$

   d) $(x^3)^4$ **e)** $(p^5)^3 \times p^2$ **f)** $c^5 \times c^{-1}$

   g) $\dfrac{l^7}{l^3}$ **h)** $\dfrac{h^8}{h^2 \times h^3}$ **i)** $\dfrac{s^3 \times s^7}{(s^2)^2 \times s}$

7   Express each of the following as a power of x:
   a) $\dfrac{x^3}{x^4}$ **b)** $\dfrac{1}{x^2}$ **c)** $\dfrac{1}{x^2} \times \dfrac{1}{x}$
   d) $x^6 \times x^{-2}$ **e)** $x^{-3} \times x^{-2}$ **f)** $x^3 \div x^{-2}$

   g) $\sqrt{x}$ **h)** $\sqrt[3]{x}$ **i)** $\sqrt{x^4}$

8   Find the value of these without using a calculator:
   a) $\sqrt{5} \times \sqrt{5}$ **b)** $\left(\sqrt{11}\right)^4$ **c)** $3^{\frac{1}{2}} \times 3^{\frac{1}{2}} \times 3^{\frac{1}{2}} \times 3^{\frac{1}{2}}$

   d) $(7.3219)^0$ **e)** 4.93×4.93^{-1} **f)** $8.75^{-1} \times 8.75^2$

9   Use a calculator to find the value of the following expressions correct to 3 S.F., given that $u = 6.31$ and $v = 0.978\,43$. You may find it helpful to store the value of v in the calculator memory.
   a) uv^2 **b)** u^2v^3 **c)** $u^2 + v^2$
   d) $(u + v)^2$ **e)** $(u - v)^3$ **f)** $u^3 - v^3$
   g) $\sqrt{u^2 + v^2}$ **h)** $\sqrt[3]{v}$ **i)** $\sqrt{u^2 - v^2}$

31.3 Standard form (1)

10 Write these numbers in standard form:

a) 57 000 000 **b)** 120 000 **c)** 231 000 000
d) 0.000 94 **e)** 0.000 000 436 **f)** 0.008
g) 57.2 × 10⁶ **h)** 0.38 × 10¹¹ **i)** 0.763 × 10⁻⁴

11 Find the value of these in standard form:

a) $(2.4 \times 10^7) \times (3 \times 10^4)$ **b)** $(8.3 \times 10^{19}) \times (4 \times 10^5)$
c) $(7.2 \times 10^8) \times 200\,000$ **d)** $(2.76 \times 10^{-3}) \times 1\,000\,000$
e) $(1.2 \times 10^{-5}) \times (3 \times 10^{-6})$ **f)** $(6.4 \times 10^9) \times (5 \times 10^{-2})$

12 Arrange the following numbers in order of size, smallest first:

a) (3.6×10^5), 58 000, (1.2×10^6), (6.7×10^5), (9.8×10^4), (4.8×10^4)
b) (7.1×10^{-6}), (4.8×10^{-5}), 0.000 072, (1.3×10^{-4}), (1.3×10^{-5})

13 Find the value of these in standard form correct to 2 S.F.

a) $(3.4 \times 10^{12}) + (5.2 \times 10^{12})$ **b)** $(7.3 \times 10^{15}) - (3.8 \times 10^{15})$
c) $(6.3 \times 10^8) + (4.7 \times 10^7)$ **d)** $(1.6 \times 10^{27}) - (8.4 \times 10^{26})$
e) $(9.7 \times 10^{-7}) + (4.5 \times 10^{-7})$ **f)** $(8.1 \times 10^{-9}) - (3.5 \times 10^{-10})$
g) $(4.5 \times 10^{24}) \div (3 \times 10^{11})$ **h)** $(7.2 \times 10^{-6}) \div (2.4 \times 10^{-16})$

MEASUREMENTS

Accuracy of measurement

A weight recorded as 63 kg, correct to the nearest kg, can be as low as 62.5 kg or nearly as high as 63.5 kg. The limits for this weight can be written as:

$$62.5 \leq x < 63.5$$

This means that there is the possibility of the recorded weight being incorrect by as much as 0.5 kg either side.

Similarly a weight recorded as 63.0 kg implies that measurements are correct to 0.1 kg. The limits in this instance are:

$$62.95 \leq x < 63.05$$

The possible error is now only 0.05 kg either side of the stated weight.

Another way of saying this is that the **lower bound** is 62.95 kg and the **upper bound** is 63.05 kg.

In general, if a measurement is accurate to some given amount, the maximum error is half of that amount.

Areas and volumes

A rectangle is measured as 12 mm long and 6 mm wide (measurement correct to the nearest mm).

The limits for the length are: $11.5 \leq l < 12.5$
The limits for the width are: $5.5 \leq w < 6.5$

The limits for the perimeter (where $p = 2l + 2w$) are:

$$(2 \times 11.5) + (2 \times 5.5) \leq p < (2 \times 12.5) + (2 \times 6.5)$$
$$34 \leq p < 38$$

So the perimeter must lie between 34 mm and 38 mm.

The limits for the area (where $a = lw$) are:

$$11.5 \times 5.5 \leq a < 12.5 \times 6.5$$
$$63.25 \leq a < 81.25$$

So the area must lie between 63.25 mm² and 81.25 mm².

For a solid shape the lower limit of the volume is found by using the smallest possible dimensions, while the upper limit is found by using the largest possible dimensions.

Measuring age

Age differs from other continuous measurements in that it is always rounded down. 'Age 16' in fact includes a range of ages from just 16 to nearly 17. Age 16 can be written as having the limits:

$16 \leq x < 17$

Similarly the true age range for ages 0–4 is:

$0 \leq x < 5$

Compound measures

Speed is the rate at which a moving object covers distance in one unit of time. It is measured in such units as km/h and m.p.h., which are called **compound measures**.

$$\text{Average speed} = \frac{\text{total distance travelled}}{\text{total time taken}}$$

$$\text{Time taken} = \frac{\text{total distance travelled}}{\text{average speed}}$$

Distance = average speed × time.

Example

A lorry travels 60 miles at an average speed of 30 m.p.h. and a further 30 miles at an average speed of 40 m.p.h. Calculate its average speed for the whole journey to one decimal place.

Answer

Time taken for first 60 miles at 30 m.p.h.

$$\text{Time} = \frac{60}{30} = 2 \text{ hours}$$

Time taken for next 30 miles at 40 m.p.h.

$$\text{Time} = \frac{30}{40} = 0.75 \text{ hours}$$

Total time taken $= 2 + 0.75 = 2.75$ hours

Total distance $= 60 + 30 = 90$ miles

Average speed $= \dfrac{90}{2.75} = 32.7$ m.p.h. (to 1 D.P.)

Questions

32.1 Accuracy of measurement

For each of the measurements given here, write down the upper and lower limits.

1 Sally weighs 55 kg.

2 Her baby brother weighs 6.3 kg.

3 This piece of string is 20 cm long.

4 The length of this leaf is 5.0 cm.

5 It will take you 7 minutes to walk into town.

6 My journey to school is 8 km.

7 Joe has measured his journey to school as 3.2 miles.

8 I can walk at a speed of 6 km/h.

9 This kitchen unit measures 900 mm across.

10 I measured the gap for the kitchen unit as 90 cm. Will it fit in?

32.2 Combined errors

11 The side of a square correct to the nearest whole number is 9 cm. Find:
a) the upper limit for the length of a side of this square
b) the smallest possible value for the length of a side
c) the upper limit for the area of this square
d) the smallest possible area.

12 The diameter of a circular flower bed is 6 m correct to the nearest metre.
Taking π as 3.14, find the upper and lower limits for:
a) its circumference
b) its area.
Give your answers to b) correct to 3 decimal places.

13 The side of a solid metal cube is 5 cm correct to the nearest mm.
Find the smallest possible volume of metal in the cube (correct to 3 decimal places).

14 a) A field is estimated to have an area of 7500 m² correct to the nearest 100 m². Give the upper and lower limits for this area.
b) The length of the field is estimated as 150 m correct to the nearest 10 m. Give the upper and lower limits for the length.
c) Use your answers to parts a) and b) to find the largest and smallest possible value for the width of the field (correct to 2 D.P.).

32.3 Measuring age

15 The table below gives the ages of children registering on a summer play scheme.

a) Copy the table and complete the true age range for each group.

b) Draw a histogram showing the true age range for each group on the horizontal axis.

c) What is the midpoint of the true age range $3 \leq x < 5$?

d) Use the true midpoint of each age group to find an estimate of the mean age of this group of children.

Age	Frequency	True age range
3–4	5	$\leq x <$
5–6	8	$\leq x <$
7–8	7	$\leq x <$
9–10	9	$\leq x <$
11–12	4	$\leq x <$
13–14	2	$\leq x <$

32.4 and 32.5 Compound measures and average speeds

16 A water tap can deliver water at the rate of $\frac{1}{2}$ litre per second. How long will it take to fill a trough which measures $70 \, \text{cm} \times 150 \, \text{cm} \times 1 \, \text{m}$?

17 A motorist leaves Bristol at 11.55 hours and arrives in Hereford $1\frac{1}{4}$ hours later. The distance from Bristol to Hereford is 50 miles.

a) At what time did she arrive in Hereford?

b) What was her average speed?

18 A boat leaves harbour at 02.35 hours and arrives at its destination at 04.05 hours. If it travels at an average speed of 9 m.p.h., how far did it go?

19 On his journey to work, Mr Smith drives 5 miles through town taking 30 minutes, followed by 16 miles on the motorway in 15 minutes. What is the average speed taken over the whole journey?

20 On a train journey of 234 km the average speed for the first 54 km was 90 km/h.

a) Find the time taken for this part of the journey.

b) For the remaining part of the journey, the average speed was 75 km/h. Find the time taken for the second part of the journey.

c) What was the total time for the whole journey?

d) What was the average speed calculated over the whole 234 km?

21 A main road through a village has a speed limit of 40 miles per hour. A motorist covers the $\frac{3}{4}$ mile section in one minute. Did he break the speed limit? Explain your answer.

CALCULATOR PROBLEMS

Standard form (with a calculator)

Scientific calculators have a special key that allows numbers to be entered directly in standard form. On most calculators this key is labelled **EXP** but on some it is labelled **EE** . The use of this key greatly extends the range of numbers that a calculator is able to work with.

Example

a) Find the value of $(2.397 \times 10^{15}) \times (6.382 \times 10^{11})$ correct to 3 S.F.

b) Calculate $(7.31 \times 10^{-24}) \div (3.49 \times 10^{-16})$ correct to 2 S.F.

Answer

a) Key this in as

2.397 **EXP** 15 **×** 6.382 **EXP** 11

giving $1.529\,765\,4 \times 10^{27} = 1.53 \times 10^{27}$ (to 3 S.F.)

Remember to write the answer using the correct notation.

b) Key this in as

7.31 **EXP** 24 **+/−** **÷** 3.49 **EXP** 16 **+/−** ⟵

*Some calculators have a special (−) key which would be pressed **before** the number is entered.*

giving $2.094\,555\,8 \times 10^{-8} = 2.1 \times 10^{-8}$ (to 2 S.F.)

Interest on savings

If the interest paid into an account is immediately withdrawn, by the account holder, then the original sum will continue to gather interest at the same rate. This form of interest payment is known as **simple interest**. For example, a monthly income account will pay the account holder a sum of money each month while leaving the original investment untouched.

Example

Calculate the simple interest paid on an investment of £15 000 at 6.08% per year for 7 years.

Answer

The amount of interest paid per year = £15 000 × 0.0608 and so the total simple interest is given by £15 000 × 0.0608 × 7 = £6384.

If the interest paid into an account is *not* withdrawn, future interest will be paid on the total amount. This form of interest payment is known as **compound interest** and gathers more quickly than simple interest because it is based on amounts that continue to grow. The scale factor approach, used in Unit 19, provides an efficient method for calculating these amounts.

Example

An initial investment of £8000 is put into an account to gather compound interest at a rate of 7.1% per year.

a) What will be the value of the investment after 5 years?

b) How much compound interest will have been paid?

Answer

The value of the investment will have grown, after 5 years, to

£8000 × 1.071 × 1.071 × 1.071 × 1.071 × 1.071 = £8000 × $(1.071)^5$.

a) The total in the account after 5 years is £11 272.94 to the nearest penny.

b) The total compound interest paid = £11 272.94 − £8000

$$= £3 272.94 \text{ to the nearest penny.}$$

Loan repayment

Loans may be taken out for many purposes and from a variety of sources. In general, the lender will make a profit by adding interest charges to the amount to be repaid. The rate of interest is always given as an **annual percentage rate** (APR) but may vary considerably from one lender to another.

Example

A finance company offers a loan of £2000 at 16% APR, to be repaid in 12 equal monthly payments of £180.45.

a) Find the total amount repaid.

b) Express the interest charges as a percentage of the loan.

Answer

a) Total repaid = £180.45 × 12 = £2 165.40

b) 2 165.4 ÷ 2000 = 1.0827

So the amount repaid is 8.27% more than was borrowed, i.e. the interest charges amount to 8.27% of the loan.

Note: the percentage calculated in b) is *less* than 16% because, as payments are made, the interest is charged on a *reducing balance*. The 8.27% figure is known as a **flat rate** and refers to the equivalent rate of interest *per year* based on the whole amount.

The flat rate is easier to work with when calculating the size of the monthly repayments and, in general, the percentage figure for the flat rate is *approximately* half of the APR figure. Using this result we can obtain a good estimate of the size of the repayments.

Example

Mike and Alison are offered £1000 for their old car in part exchange for one priced at £6995 at a garage. They accept the offer and pay an extra £1495 as a deposit.

a) What is the balance to be repaid?

b) If interest is charged at 23.8% APR, and they take three years to complete the payments, approximately how much will they have to pay each month?

c) What is the total credit price for the car?

Answer

a) Part exchange value + deposit = £2495   Balance remaining = £4500

b) Flat rate $\approx \frac{1}{2} \times 23.8\% = 11.9\%$

Interest charged $\approx 11.9\% \times 3 = 35.7\%$

Total paid in instalments $\approx £4500 \times 1.357 = £6\,106.50$

Monthly payment $\approx £6\,106.50 \div 36 = £169.625 \approx £170$.

c) Total credit price = $£2495 + £6\,106.50 = £8\,601.50 \approx £8600$

The *exact* value of a monthly loan repayment may be found using the formula given below.

Using $£L = $ loan

$\qquad n = $ number of payments needed to repay loan

$$R = \sqrt[12]{1 + \frac{APR}{100}}$$

Each payment is given by $\dfrac{LR^n(R-1)}{R^n - 1}$.

Questions

33.1 Standard form (2)

1 Find the value of each of the following, in standard form, correct to 3 S.F.

    a) $537\,000 \times 239\,000\,000$ **b)** $96\,000 \times 441\,000 \times 8700$

    c) $47\,126 \times (1268)^2$ **d)** $(714)^2 \times (326)^3$

    e) $0.000003 \div 871\,000$ **f)** 0.000007×0.000412

    g) $(0.00361)^3$ **h)** $(0.23)^{20}$

2 Calculate the value of these in standard form to an accuracy of 3 S.F.

    a) $(6.72 \times 10^8) \times (3.29 \times 10^6)$ **b)** $(4.47 \times 10^{12}) \times (8.67 \times 10^9)$

    c) $(5.65 \times 10^{11}) + (9.73 \times 10^{10})$ **d)** $(1.34 \times 10^{18}) - (8.94 \times 10^{17})$

    e) $(2.76 \times 10^{-17}) \times (5.38 \times 10^{-3})$ **f)** $(4.12 \times 10^{-6}) \div (3.81 \times 10^{-15})$

    g) $(7.62 \times 10^5) \div (6.36 \times 10^{21})$ **h)** $(5.34 \times 10^{-9}) - (8.71 \times 10^{-10})$

3 Find the value of $(3.18 \times 10^8) + (9.73 \times 10^{-8})$ correct to 3 S.F.
What happens? Explain why.

4 The river Amazon flows into the Atlantic Ocean at an average rate of $124\,000\,\text{m}^3$ per second. Find the volume of water it discharges in one year correct to 2 S.F. Explain why you do not need to take account of leap years.

5 In 1890 a method was devised for finding the diameter of a molecule of oil. The assumption made was that a drop of oil would spread across the surface of water to make a layer one molecule thick. The diameter of a molecule would then be given by the depth of the oil film.

a) Using V to represent the volume of oil, A to represent the area covered and d to represent the depth of the oil film, explain why $V = Ad$.

b) Make d the subject of the formula given in a).

c) In an experiment, a drop of oil of volume $1 \times 10^{-4}\,\text{cm}^3$ is found to spread across an area of $1976\,\text{cm}^2$. Use this result to calculate the diameter of a molecule of oil to 1 S.F.

33.2 Interest on savings

6 Find the simple interest gained on £4500 invested for five years at 5.9% per year.

7 How much simple interest would be paid on £30\,000 invested for 6 months at 8.1% per year?

8 A lottery winner invests £4\,000\,000 in an account intending to 'live off the interest'. If the interest is paid at 0.83% per month, how much of a monthly income does this provide? How much interest would be paid over a period of ten years?

9 A sum of £6000 is put into an account to gather compound interest at the rate of 8.4% per year. How much money will the account contain after seven years? How much compound interest will have been accrued (gathered)?

10 Calculate the value of the compound interest accrued on £2500 invested for 10 years at 8.6% per annum.

11 a) After how many years will an initial investment of £1000 more than double in value if it gathers compound interest at 7.4% per annum?

b) What if the amount invested is £5000?

12 Find a formula for the value of an initial investment of £x after n years assuming a compound interest rate of 6.8% per annum. How many years would it take for the value to exceed £$2x$?

33.3 Loan repayment

13 A car is advertised at a price of £7995 at a garage which offers finance at 28.4% APR.

Use the approximate flat rate value to calculate the size of the monthly instalments, to the nearest £10, based on repaying the loan in 3 years and assuming a deposit of £995.

Find the total credit price of the car to the nearest £100.

14 A shop offers a video outfit comprising camcorder and accessories, together with a video recorder, for £1195 on a special 'no deposit' deal at 34.6% APR over 24 months.

Use the approximate flat rate value to calculate the total credit price of the outfit to the nearest £10. How much is each monthly repayment to the nearest £1?

15 Use the loan repayment formula to calculate the monthly repayments, to the nearest penny, on a personal loan of £5600 taken out over 4 years. How much is repaid altogether?

CUMULATIVE FREQUENCY

The interquartile range

The interquartile range is given by:

Interquartile range = value of third quartile − value of first quartile

The interquartile range tells you how much variation there is among the middle 50% of a group.

To calculate the interquartile range you need to find the first quartile (or lower quartile) which occurs one quarter of the way through the data. Likewise the third (or upper quartile) is a value three quarters of the way through the data.

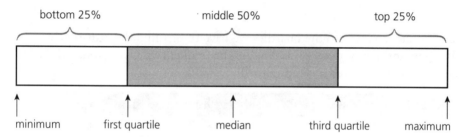

It may help to find the median (the middle value) first. Then:
■ the first quartile is halfway through the first half
■ the third quartile is halfway through the second half.

Example

Find the median and quartiles of these pupils' heights (in cm):

163   159   154   170   168   175   164   168   173   162

Answer

First arrange them in order:

154   159   162   163   164   168   168   170   173   175

first quartile   median = 166 cm   third quartile

The interquartile range = 170 − 162 = 8 cm

Another easy way to do this is to arrange your *ordered* results in the shape of a 'W'. Each section of the 'W' must contain the same number of numbers.

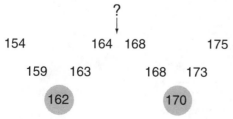

The median is at the middle of the W and the quartiles at the bottom.

So as before the median is 166 cm, the first quartile 162 cm and the third quartile 170 cm.

Cumulative frequency graphs

Pupils in a year 11 class were asked, 'How long does your journey to school take you?' Here are their answers organised into a frequency table.

Time taken in minutes	Frequency
$0 \leq x < 5$	3
$5 \leq x < 10$	4
$10 \leq x < 15$	13
$15 \leq x < 20$	7
$20 \leq x < 25$	2
$25 \leq x < 30$	1

To find the median and the quartiles we have to first find the **cumulative frequencies**. This is done by adding up the frequencies as we go down the table (sometimes called a running total).

Time	Frequency	Cumulative frequency	Times less than
$0 \leq x < 5$	3	3	5
$5 \leq x < 10$	4	7	10
$10 \leq x < 15$	13	20	15
$15 \leq x < 20$	7	27	20
$20 \leq x < 25$	2	29	25
$25 \leq x < 30$	1	30	30

The last column gives the upper limit for each class interval (group).

So there are 3 pupils with journeys less than 5 minutes, and 7 with journeys less than 10 minutes, and so on.

The next step is to draw a cumulative frequency graph. Each point is plotted by:
x coordinate = upper limit for each group
y coordinate = cumulative frequency

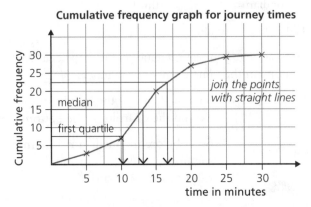

Cumulative frequency graph for journey times

The median is found by drawing a line half way up the cumulative frequency (at 15) across to the graph. The median is read off the time axis as 13 minutes.

The first quartile is found quarter of the way up the cumulative frequency (at $\frac{1}{4}$ of 30 which is $7\frac{1}{2}$). Drawing a line across at $7\frac{1}{2}$ gives the first quartile as $10\frac{1}{2}$ minutes.

Likewise draw another line three quarters of the way up at $22\frac{1}{2}$ in order to read the third quartile off the graph. This gives 17 minutes.

Interquartile range $= 17 - 10\frac{1}{2} = 6\frac{1}{2}$ minutes.

The amount of variation among the middle 50% of pupils' journeys is $6\frac{1}{2}$ minutes.

Grouped discrete data

The cumulative frequency graph drawn in the previous section is for continuous data (obtained by measuring).

For continuous data, the value of the cumulative frequency tells you how many results are *less than* the upper boundary of each class interval.

It is also possible to draw a cumulative frequency graph for grouped discrete data (results which were originally obtained by counting).

For discrete data the cumulative frequency gives the number of results which are *less than or equal to* the upper boundary of each class interval.

Questions

34.1 and 34.2 Median and interquartile range

1   Richard is doing a survey on transport. He has counted the number of passengers on buses stopping at bus-stops near the library one Saturday morning between 10 am and 10.30 am.

Buses going towards town centre
16   12   15   25   29   13   18   20

Buses going away from town centre
5   3   0   2   9   8   6   11   5

a) Find the median and interquartile range for buses going in each direction.
b) Can you think of a reason for the big differences in the two sets of results?

2   Three classes take the same Maths test. Find the range, median, first quartile, third quartile and and interquartile range for each class.

Class X
15 18 11 9 13 14 16 20 18 17 9 15 14 18 7 17 19

Class Y
10 11 12 16 17 9 8 12 13 11 11 13 10 9 9 6 16 12 14

Class Z
17 18 16 17 5 15 20 20 19 18 16 14 15 12 20 20 19 19 18 17 13

3   Lizzie has been asked to do a survey of first-class and second-class letters arriving at the school office. By looking at the postmark she can tell how long each letter has taken to be delivered. Find the median and interquartile range for:
a) first-class   **b)** second-class.

Delivery in working days	Number of letters	
	First-class	Second-class
1	19	3
2	5	18
3	2	12
4	0	5
5	0	0
6	0	0
7	0	0
8	0	1
9	1	0
10	0	2

Write a couple of sentences about the delivery times for first-class and second-class post.

34.3 and 34.4 Cumulative frequency graphs

4   The cumulative frequency graph opposite shows the birth weights of 225 babies born in a particular hospital. (Their weights were measured in kg.)
a) Find the median weight of these babies.
b) Find the interquartile range.
c) If possible, find out your birth weight. (If you are told your weight in pounds and ounces you can use 1 lb = 16 oz and 1 kg = 2.2 lbs.)
    Where does your birth weight appear on this graph?
    How many of these babies would weigh less than you did?

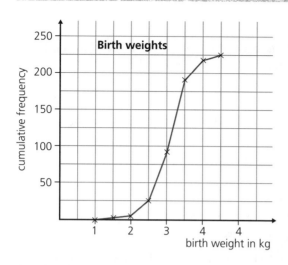

5 Our local supermarket sells crisps in packets labelled 25 g e. The e means that the mean (average) weight of all the packets must be 25 g. We weighed some packets using an electronic balance in the science laboratory.

a) Work out the cumulative frequency column.
b) Draw a cumulative frequency graph.
c) Find the median weight.
d) Find the interquartile range.

Weight (g)	Frequency
$24.8 \leq x < 25.0$	3
$25.0 \leq x < 25.2$	12
$25.2 \leq x < 25.4$	16
$25.4 \leq x < 25.6$	5
$25.6 \leq x < 25.8$	3
$25.8 \leq x < 26.0$	1

6 Sally asked people to guess the amount of time for a 1 minute interval. She had a stopwatch to help her time and record their estimate.

True time estimated in s	Frequency
$20 \leq x < 30$	4
$30 \leq x < 40$	15
$40 \leq x < 50$	21
$50 \leq x < 60$	26
$60 \leq x < 70$	13
$70 \leq x < 80$	4
$80 \leq x < 90$	1

a) How many people took part in Sally's experiment?
b) Find the cumulative frequencies.
c) Draw the cumulative frequency graph.
d) Find the interquartile range and the median.
e) Do you think people were good at estimating one minute?

FURTHER EQUATIONS

Manipulating equations

The balancing approach to solving equations, considered earlier, can also be used to change the form of an equation to suit a particular purpose.

Example

Show that the graph of the equation $2y - 3x = 8$ is a straight line and find its gradient and y-intercept.

Answer

$2y - 3x = 8$ *Add 3x to both sides of the equation.*
$2y = 3x + 8$ *Divide both sides by 2.*
              Note that $(3x + 8) \div 2 = \frac{1}{2}(3x + 8) = 1.5x + 4$ giving
$y = 1.5x + 4$ *which is in the form $y = mx + c$.*

It follows that the graph is a straight line with gradient 1.5 and y-intercept at 4.

The ability to manipulate an equation allows us to rearrange a formula to provide us with new information. This means, for example, that we only need to remember one version of a formula, knowing that it can be adapted to suit a particular problem.

The *subject* of the formula $v = u + at$ is v since it takes the form $v = ...$

Example

Rearrange the formula $v = u + at$ so that a is the subject.

Answer

$v = u + at$ *Subtract u from both sides so that the term containing a is isolated.*

$v - u = at$ *Divide both sides by t.*

$\dfrac{v - u}{t} = a$, i.e. $a = \dfrac{v - u}{t}$ *The subject is normally written on the left-hand side of the equation.*

Simultaneous equations (substitution method)

Example

Solve the simultaneous equations $x + y = 8$ and $y = x + 2$.

Answer

$x + y = 8$ (1)
    $y = x + 2$ (2)

Using equation (2), we can re-write equation (1) by replacing y with $x + 2$, i.e. we can *substitute* for y in equation (1).

This gives:

$$x + (x + 2) = 8 \qquad \textit{Remove the brackets and simplify.}$$
$$2x + 2 = 8$$
$$2x = 6$$
$$x = 3$$

Substituting for x in equation (2) gives $y = 5$. The required solution is $x = 3$ and $y = 5$.
(*Check*: substituting for x and y in equation (1) gives $x + y = 3 + 5 = 8$.)

In some situations it may be necessary to rearrange an equation to make one of the letters the subject so that the substitution can be made.

Example

Solve the equations $2q - 3p = 2$ and $q - p = 3$.

Answer

$$2q - 3p = 2 \qquad (1)$$
$$q - p = 3 \qquad (2) \qquad \textit{Equation (2) is easily rearranged to make q the subject.}$$

From (2), $q = p + 3$ (3)

Substituting for q in (1) gives
$$2(p + 3) - 3p = 2$$
$$2p + 6 - 3p = 2$$
$$-p + 6 = 2$$
$$-p = -4$$
$$p = 4$$

Substituting for p in (3) gives $q = 7$ and so the solution is $p = 4$ and $q = 7$.
(*Check*: substituting for p and q in (1) gives $2q - 3p = 2 \times 7 - 3 \times 4 = 2$.)

Multiplying linear expressions

Example

Expand and simplify:
a) $(x + 4)(x + 1)$ b) $(x + 2)(x - 3)$ c) $(x - 5)(x + 1)$ d) $(x - 5)^2$

Answer

a) $(x + 4)(x + 1) = x(x + 1) + 4(x + 1)$
$$= x^2 + x + 4x + 4$$
$$= x^2 + 5x + 4$$

b) $(x + 2)(x - 3) = x(x - 3) + 2(x - 3) = x^2 - 3x + 2x - 6 = x^2 - x - 6$

c) $(x - 5)(x + 1) = x(x + 1) - 5(x + 1) = x^2 + x - 5x - 5 = x^2 - 4x - 5$

d) $(x - 5)^2 = (x - 5)(x - 5) = x^2 - 5x - 5x + 25 = x^2 - 10x + 25$

Highest common factor

Example

Given that $360 = 2^3 \times 3^2 \times 5$, $432 = 2^4 \times 3^3$ and $540 = 2^2 \times 3^3 \times 5$, find the highest common factor of all three numbers.

Answer

All three numbers contain a factor of 2^2 and a factor of 3^2 but only two of the numbers contain a factor of 5. The highest common factor therefore is $2^2 \times 3^2 = 36$.

Example

Factorise $a^2x^3 + a^3x$.

Answer

$a^2x^3 + a^3x = a^2x(x^2 + a)$ *Treating the letters in the same way as the prime factors in the first example, we see that the highest common factor of the two terms is a^2x.*

Note: $a^2x \times x^2 = a^2x^3$ and $a^2x \times a = a^3x$.

Questions

35.1 Manipulating equations

1 Write the following equations in the form $y = mx + c$.
   a) $2y = 6x + 10$ b) $5y = 10x - 15$ c) $2.5y = 5x + 7.5$
   d) $y - x = 11$ e) $y + 6.2 = 4x$ f) $2y - 10x = 8$
   g) $y + x = 5$ h) $4x + 2y = 9$ i) $2x - 3y + 1 = 0$

2 Which of the following equations represent lines which cross the y-axis at $(0, -3)$?
   a) $y - 3 = 2x$ b) $2y = 5x - 6$ c) $y = -3x + 3$
   d) $y + 3 = -3x$ e) $1.5y = 6x - 4.5$ f) $y + 2x - 3 = 0$

3 Make x the subject of each of these equations:
   a) $px = q$ b) $x + p = q$ c) $q = p - x$
   d) $px + q = r$ e) $p(x + q) = r$ f) $p - (q - x) = r$

   g) $\dfrac{x}{p} = q$ h) $\dfrac{x}{p + q} = r$ i) $\dfrac{x}{p} + q = r$

   j) $\dfrac{px}{q} = r$ k) $\dfrac{x - p}{q} = r$ l) $\dfrac{x + p}{q} - r = 0$

4 a) Make a the subject of the formula $F = m(g + a)$.
   b) Find the value of a given that $F = 50$, $m = 2.5$ and $g = 9.8$.

5 **a)** Make l the subject of the formula $T = 2\pi\sqrt{\dfrac{l}{g}}$.

    b) Find the value of l given that $T = 4.71$, $\pi = 3.14$ and $g = 10$.

35.2 Simultaneous equations

6 Solve these equations using the substitution method:

    a) $2p + q = 24$ **b)** $j + 2k = 19$ **c)** $u - 4v = 1$
        $q = p + 3$ $k = j - 7$ $v + 7 = u$

    d) $2t - 4s = 3$ **e)** $2x + 3y = 7$ **f)** $a + 2v = 2$
        $t - s = 6$ $x + y = 5$ $a = v - 7$

    g) $3n - 2m = 4$ **h)** $2k - 3l = 25$
        $m = n - 3$ $k - l = 5$

7 Solve the following equations by the method of your choice:

    a) $5y + z = 14$ **b)** $k = 4g - 3$
        $2y + z = 5$ $g + k = 7$

    c) $25t - 300 = s$ **d)** $8x - 11y = 310$
        $10t + s = 400$ $3x + 11y = -35$

35.3 Multiplying linear expressions

8 Expand and simplify each of the following expressions:

    a) $(x + 5)(x + 3)$ **b)** $(x + 2)(x + 7)$ **c)** $(x + 8)(x + 10)$
    d) $(n + 6)(n + 4)$ **e)** $(g + 11)(g + 9)$ **f)** $(k + 7)(k + 20)$
    g) $(2x + 3)(x + 2)$ **h)** $(a + 4)(3a + 1)$ **i)** $(2w + 1)(4w + 3)$
    j) $(x + 7)^2$ **k)** $(p + 4)^2$ **l)** $(h + 10)^2$
    m) $(3x + 1)^2$ **n)** $(5w + 4)^2$ **o)** $(1 + 6t)^2$

9 Expand and simplify:

    a) $(x - 3)(x + 7)$ **b)** $(y - 4)(y + 11)$ **c)** $(p - 6)(p + 6)$
    d) $(d - 7)(d + 3)$ **e)** $(x - 8)(x + 1)$ **f)** $(t - 10)(t + 9)$
    g) $(f + 5)(f - 2)$ **h)** $(h + 1)(h - 5)$ **i)** $(x + 4)(x - 11)$
    j) $(x - 3)(x - 6)$ **k)** $(2x - 4)(x - 3)$ **l)** $(3x - 4)^2$

10 **a)** Show that this rectangle has the same perimeter as one that is x cm wide and $(x + 7)$ cm long.

    b) Find the difference in their areas. Does this answer depend on the value of x?

$(x + 1)$ cm

$(x + 6)$ cm

35.4 Highest common factor

11 Find the highest common factor of $5^3 \times 7^2$ and 2×5^2.

12 Given that $p = 3^2 \times 5^3 \times 11$, $q = 3^3 \times 5 \times 7^2$ and $r = 3 \times 5^2 \times 7 \times 11$, find the highest common factors of each of the following:

a) p and q **b)** q and r **c)** p, q and r

d) q and $3r$ **e)** p and $25q$ **f)** p and 150

13 Factorise these expressions fully:

a) $x^2y + xy^2$ **b)** $pqr - qrt$ **c)** $8x + 12y$

d) $5uv - 10u$ **e)** $12hk - 9h^2$ **f)** $14cd + 7d$

g) $a^2b + ab^2 + ab$ **h)** $wz^2 - w^2z + wz^3$ **i)** $9xy^2 - 12x^2y + 15xy$

We say that:

Length is a measurement in one dimension.

Area is a measurement in two dimensions.

Volume is a measurement in three dimensions.

Mathematically speaking:

The dimension of length or perimeter is L.

The dimension of area is $L \times L = L^2$.

The dimension of volume is $L \times L \times L = L^3$.

We can use this simple idea to check formulae.

Example

This is a test tube. Check the dimension of each of the expressions given here and decide which ones might be a formula for:
a) the surface area
b) the volume.

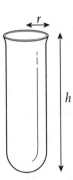

   (i) $2\pi rh$ (ii) $\frac{2}{3}\pi r + \pi r^2 h$ (iii) $2\pi r^2 h^2$

  (iv) $\frac{2}{3}\pi r^3 + \pi r^2 h$ (v) $\frac{2}{3}\pi r^3 r + \pi r^2 h$ (vi) $2\pi h$

Answer

Note that π does not have a 'dimension'. It has a constant value and does not affect the dimension of a formula. Likewise any number such as 2 or 6 or $\frac{2}{3}$ is dimension-less.

The dimensions for each expression are:

  (i) $2\pi rh$ number × number × length × length $= L^2$

 (ii) $\frac{2}{3}\pi r + \pi r^2 h$ number × number × length + number × length² × length
                                            $= L + L^3$

(iii) $2\pi r^2 h^2$ number × number × length² × length² $= L^4$

(iv) $\frac{2}{3}\pi r^3 + \pi r^2 h$ number × number × length³ + number × length² × length
                                          $= L^3 + L^3 = L^3$

 (v) $\frac{2}{3}\pi r^3 r + \pi r^2 h$ number × number × length + number × length² × length
                                          $= L + L^3$

(vi) $2\pi h$ number × number × length $= L$

(Note that any expressions with mixed dimensions such as number (ii) or number (v) simply do not make sense and are impossible.)

a) A formula for surface area must have dimension L^2.
   Expression (i) is the only one with these dimensions.
b) A formula for volume must have dimension L^3.
   Expression (iv) is the only one with these dimensions.

The dimension method does not tell you if the formula is correct, but it could tell you if it is impossible.

Introducing the tangent

The tangent can be used to find the height of a right-angled triangle. The height is given by:

height = $x \times \tan \theta$.

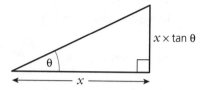

Example

Find y, the height of this right-angled triangle.

Answer

$y = 8 \times \tan 27° = 4.076$

So the height is 4.1 cm (correct to 1 D.P.)

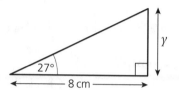

Questions

36.1 Checking with dimensions

1   Which formula for the surface area of this pyramid is correct?
Find the dimensions of each of these formulae, in order to find the correct one.

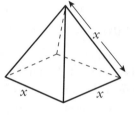

a) x^3 b) $x^2 + 4x$ c) $x^2 + \sqrt{3}\,x^2$
d) $x^3 + \sqrt{3}\,x^2$ e) $8x$

2   The length of metal framework needed to make this ice-hockey goal is given by:

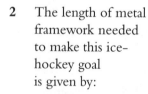

a) $\dfrac{\pi x^2}{2} + 2y$

b) $12xy + \pi x$

c) $4x + 3y + \pi x^2$

d) $4x + 3y + \pi x$

e) $12\pi xy$

3   The volume of air enclosed inside the ice-hockey goal is:

a) $\dfrac{\pi x^2 y}{4}$ b) $\dfrac{\pi x^2}{4} + y$ c) $2\pi^2 xy$ d) $12\pi xy$

4 The area of card needed to make this rocket shape is given by:

a) $2\pi r^2 l + 2\pi R^2 L + 2\pi Rr$

b) $\pi R^2 - \pi r^2 + 2\pi rl + \pi RL$

c) $\pi R^2(R + L) + 2\pi r^2(r + l)$

d) $2\pi r + \pi RL$

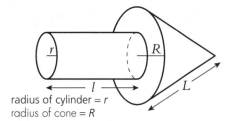

radius of cylinder = r
radius of cone = R

36.2 Pictorial representations

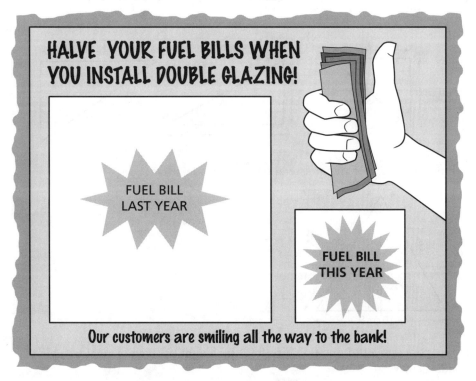

5 a) Measure the size of last year's fuel bill and find its area.
   b) Measure the size of this year's fuel bill as it is shown in the picture and find its area.
   c) Explain why the picture in this advert is misleading.
   d) Draw your own version of this advert. Explain why your own version is correct.

36.3 Introducing the tangent

6 Find the value *y* in each triangle.

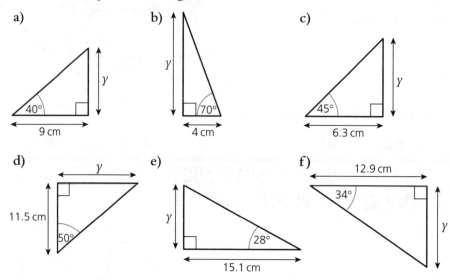

a)

b)

c)

d)

e)

f)

7 Find the height of an equilateral triangle of side 10 cm.

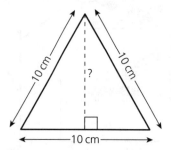

8 Use your answer to question 7 to find the height of an equilateral triangle of side 1 cm.

9 The angle of elevation to the top of a tree is 36° when measured from a position 30 m from the base of the tree. How tall is the tree?

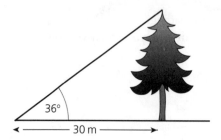

Plotting, drawing and solving

By plotting a sufficient number of points, it is possible to draw the graph of an equation with enough accuracy to solve related equations. The fact that equations can be rearranged in different ways shows that we have a choice over which graphs to use in order to locate the solutions.

Example

Use the graph of $y = x^2$ together with an appropriate straight line graph to solve the equation $x^2 - 7x + 9 = 0$.

Answer

$$x^2 - 7x + 9 = 0 \qquad \textit{Add 7x to both sides of the equation.}$$
$$x^2 + 9 = 7x \qquad \textit{Subtract 9 from both sides.}$$
$$x^2 = 7x - 9 \qquad \textit{This shows that the solutions may be found at the points where the graphs of } y = x^2 \textit{ and } y = 7x - 9 \textit{ intersect.}$$

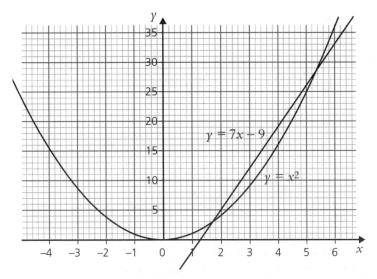

From the graph, the solutions are $x = 1.7$ and $x = 5.3$ to 1 D.P.

(*Note:* the values of x at which graphs of $y = x^2$ and $y = 7x - 9$ intersect are the same as those at which the graph of $y = x^2 - 7x + 9$ crosses the x-axis, as you can check on page 350 of the classbook.)

The instruction to **draw** the graph of an equation means that an accurate diagram is required. Typically this may then be used to obtain further information by reading off appropriate values. However, the instruction to **sketch** the graph of an equation means that the diagram need only show the graph's main features, such as its shape and where it crosses the coordinate axes.

37 Algebra and graphs (3)

Example

Sketch the graph of the equation $y = (x + 2)(x - 3)$.

Answer

When $x = 0$, $y = (0 + 2)(0 - 3) = -6$.　　*It follows that the curve crosses the y-axis at (0, −6).*

$y = 0$ when $x = -2$ and when $x = 3$.　　*It follows that the curve crosses the x-axis at (−2, 0) and at (3, 0).*

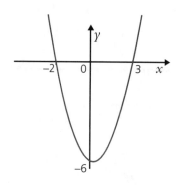

*Since the equation would take the form $y = ax^2 + bx + c$ if the brackets were removed, with $a > 0$, the shape of the curve is a **parabola**.*

An equation of the form $y = ax^3 + bx^2 + cx + d$ (where $a \neq 0$) is called a **cubic** equation. The highest power of x in such an equation is 3.

Each of these is a cubic equation:
$y = x^3$
$y = 2x^3$
$y = x^3 - 5$
$y = 4x^3 + 2x$
$y = x^3 - 6x^2 + x + 1$

The following are **not** cubic equations:
$y = x^2 + 3x$　　(the highest power of x is 2)
$y = x^4 - 2x^3$　　(the highest power of x is 4)
$y = x^3 + x^{-1}$　　(the equation includes a *negative* power of x)

For $a > 0$ the graph of a cubic equation takes one of these forms:

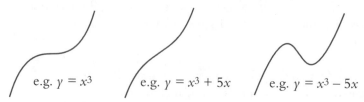

e.g. $y = x^3$　　　e.g. $y = x^3 + 5x$　　　e.g. $y = x^3 - 5x$

Inequalities in two dimensions

The set of points that satisfy an equation such as $x + y = 4$ may be represented by a line. On one side of the line the values of $x + y$ are *always* larger than 4 and on the other side of the line the values of $x + y$ are *always* smaller than 4. In this way, the line $x + y = 4$ divides the plane into two parts, known as **regions**, defined by the inequalities $x + y < 4$ and $x + y > 4$.

The line itself may be described as a **boundary line** for the two regions. Note that the boundary line is shown dashed because the points on it are not included in the region. A solid line is used to represent the region given by $x + y \geq 4$.

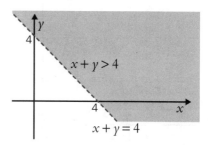

The technique of using graphs to solve equations may be adapted to find the solution of inequalities.

Example

Use this diagram to find the values of x for which the following are true:

a) $x^2 - 3x < 2$ b) $x^2 - 3x \geq 2$

Answer

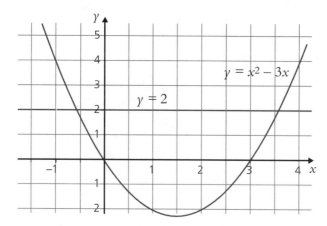

a) The graph of $y = x^2 - 3x$ intersects the graph of $y = 2$ when $x = -0.6$ and when $x = 3.6$, but lies below it for values in between. Hence, the solution of $x^2 - 3x < 2$ is $-0.6 < x < 3.6$ (correct to 1 D.P.)

b) The solution of $x^2 - 3x \geq 2$ must be written in two parts as $x \leq -0.6$ or $x \geq 3.6$ (correct to 1 D.P.)

Questions

37.1 Plotting, drawing and solving

1   This diagram shows the graph of $y = x^3 - 6x$.

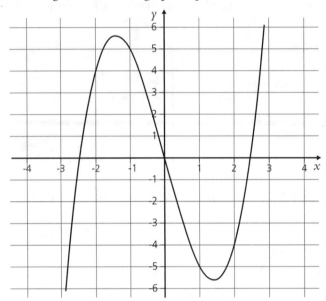

Use the graph to find the values of x, correct to 1 D.P., that satisfy the following equations:

a) $x^3 - 6x = 6$ b) $x^3 - 6x = 4$ c) $x^3 - 6x = -3$

d) $x^3 = 6x - 7$ e) $x^3 + 2x = 8x$ f) $x(x^2 - 6) = 5$

2   Given that the graph of $y = 3x^2$ has been drawn, state the equations of the lines that could be added to the diagram to solve these equations.

a) $3x^2 = 11$ b) $3x^2 - 7 = 0$ c) $3x^2 - 10 = 0$

d) $3x^2 - 5x = 4$ e) $3x^2 - 2x + 3 = 0$ f) $x^2 - 5x = x(3 - 2x)$

3   Draw the graph of $y = \dfrac{10}{x^2}$ for values of x from -5 to 5 (not including zero).

Use the graph together with any extra lines as necessary to solve the following equations to 1 D.P.

a) $\dfrac{10}{x^2} = 5$ b) $\dfrac{10}{x^2} - 1 = 0$ c) $\dfrac{10}{x^2} = x$

4   Sketch the graphs of the following equations:

a) $y = (x - 1)(x - 5)$ b) $y = (x - 2)(x - 3)$ c) $y = (x + 3)(x - 2)$

d) $y = (x + 4)(x + 8)$ e) $y = x(x - 6)$ f) $y = x(x + 3)$

g) $y = x^2 + 7x$ h) $y = (x - 4)^2$ i) $y = (x + 3)^2$

5   Sketch the graph of $y = x(x + 2)(x - 3)$.

37.2 Inequalities in two dimensions

6 Draw diagrams to show the regions given by the following inequalities:

a) $x > 3$ **b)** $x \leq -2$ **c)** $y < 1$

d) $y \geq -3$ **e)** $0 \leq x \leq 4$ **f)** $-1 \leq x < 2$

g) $-5 < y \leq 0$ **h)** $1 < y < 5$

7 Draw diagrams to represent these inequalities:

a) $y \geq x + 1$ **b)** $x + y < 5$ **c)** $x + y \geq -6$ **d)** $2x + y \leq 8$

8 Use inequalities to describe the shaded regions in the diagrams below.

a)

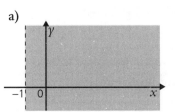

b)

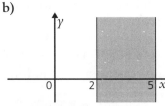

c)

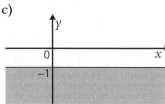

d)

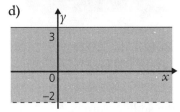

e)

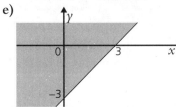

f)

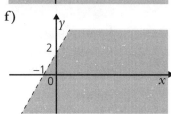

9 Use this diagram to solve these inequalities:

a) $(x + 3)(x - 2) \leq 0$ **b)** $(x + 3)(x - 2) \geq 0$

c) $(x + 3)(x - 2) < 4$ **d)** $x^2 + x - 8 > 0$

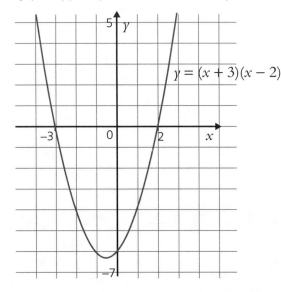

$y = (x + 3)(x - 2)$

38 COMBINING PROBABILITIES

Mutually exclusive events.

Events which cannot happen at the same time are called **mutually exclusive events.**

When this spinner is spun, the arrow may stop in any one of the sections numbered 1 to 8.

If event A is 'the arrow stops at an even number' and event B is 'the arrow stops on number 5' then events A and B are mutually exclusive.

The **addition principle** can be used to find the probability for mutually exclusive events happening.

> If two events A and B are mutually exclusive, the probability of event A or event B happening can be found by **adding** the probabilities.
>
> P(A or B) = P(A) + P(B)

Example

If event A is 'the arrow stops at an even number' and event B is 'the arrow stops on number 5', what is the probability of event A *or* event B happening?

Answer
The probability of event A or event B is found by using the addition principle:

P(A or B) = P(A) + P(B)

$P(A) = \dfrac{4}{8}$, $P(B) = \dfrac{1}{8}$

$P(A \text{ or } B) = \dfrac{4}{8} + \dfrac{1}{8} = \dfrac{5}{8}$

Example

If I pick a card from a shuffled pack of cards, what is the probability that I pick a King (of any suit) or the Queen of hearts?

Answer
Using the addition principal:

$P(\text{any King}) = \dfrac{4}{52}$

$P(\text{Queen of hearts}) = \dfrac{1}{52}$

$P(\text{any King or the Queen of hearts}) = \dfrac{4}{52} + \dfrac{1}{52} = \dfrac{5}{52}$

Independent events

Two events are **independent** if the outcome of the second event is not
affected by the outcome of the first.

If there is some influence or changing of probabilities, then the events are not
independent.

Consider these two events.

Event A

> The postman delivers
> the mail before 8 am

Event B

> I have toast for breakfast

These events are independent (providing I do not rely on the postman to
wake me up in good time to make the toast!).

The **multiplication principle** can be used to find the probability of
independent events happening together.

> If events A and B are independent, the probability of both A and B
> happening together can be found by **multiplying** the separate
> probabilities for A and B.
>
> P(A and B) = P(A) × P(B)

Example

A dice is thrown twice. What is the probability of obtaining a six on the
first throw followed by a score of five or higher on the second throw?

Answer

The events are independent. Using the multiplication principle:

$P(\text{six}) = \dfrac{1}{6}$

$P(\text{five or higher}) = \dfrac{2}{6} = \dfrac{1}{3}$

$P(\text{six on first throw and score five or higher on second throw}) = \dfrac{1}{6} \times \dfrac{1}{3} = \dfrac{1}{18}$

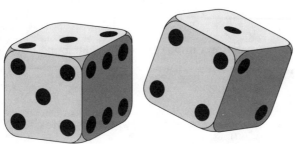

38 Combining probabilities

Tree diagrams

If two complex events are to happen together, all the possible outcomes can be shown on a table or on a **tree diagram**.

A tree diagram can be extended to show the outcomes of three events by adding further branches. The probabilities of combined outcomes are found by multiplying the probabilities following the branches on the tree.

Example

Alice has recently taken up archery. At the moment the probability that she hits the target is $\frac{1}{3}$. What is the probability that she will hit the target at least once, if she fires two arrows?

Answer

(*Note*: we have to assume that Alice's two shots are independent and that the probability of a 'hit' remains the same at $\frac{1}{3}$.)

First arrow	Second arrow	Outcome	Probability
	$\frac{1}{3}$ hit	H,H	$\frac{1}{3} \times \frac{1}{3} = \frac{1}{9}$
$\frac{1}{3}$ hit	$\frac{2}{3}$ miss	H,M	$\frac{1}{3} \times \frac{2}{3} = \frac{2}{9}$
	$\frac{1}{3}$ hit	M,H	$\frac{2}{3} \times \frac{1}{3} = \frac{2}{9}$
$\frac{2}{3}$ miss	$\frac{2}{3}$ miss	M,M	$\frac{2}{3} \times \frac{2}{3} = \frac{4}{9}$

Of the four possible outcomes, there are three which will give Alice at least one hit.

$$P(H, H) = \frac{1}{3} \times \frac{1}{3} = \frac{1}{9}$$

$$P(H, M) = \frac{1}{3} \times \frac{2}{3} = \frac{2}{9}$$

$$P(M, H) = \frac{2}{3} \times \frac{1}{3} = \frac{2}{9}$$

These are all mutually exclusive outcomes and so their probabilities can be added together (the addition principle):

$$P \text{ (at least one hit)} = \frac{1}{9} + \frac{2}{9} + \frac{2}{9} = \frac{5}{9}$$

Alternatively the same solution can be reached by subtracting P(no hits) from 1.

$$P(\text{no hits}) = P(M, M) = \frac{4}{9}$$

$$P(\text{at least one hit}) = 1 - P(\text{no hits})$$

$$= 1 - \frac{4}{9} = \frac{5}{9}$$

Questions

38.1 and 38.2 Mutually exclusive events and the addition principle

1   Which of these events are mutually exclusive?
  a) I throw an ordinary six-sided dice.
       Event A: I score an even number.
       Event B: I score a six.
  b) I throw an ordinary six-sided dice.
       Event A: I score an even number.
       Event B: I score a prime number.
  c) Two babies are born at the hospital today.
       Event A: both babies are girls.
       Event B: at least one baby is a girl.
  d) Two babies are born at the hospital today.
       Event A: both babies are girls.
       Event B: one baby is a boy, the other is a girl.

2   Find the probability that I score a total of 11 or 12 if I throw 2 dice.

3   For breakfast Daniel always has either cornflakes or Weetabix or toast.
   The probability that he has cornflakes is $\frac{3}{5}$ and the probability that he has
   toast is $\frac{3}{10}$.
   a) What is the probability that he has Weetabix?
   b) What is the probability that he has Weetabix or cornflakes?

4   My computer can be programmed to generate random numbers between 0
   and 9. What is the probability that the next number it generates is:
   a) a prime number
   b) an odd number
   c) an odd number which is not prime
   d) a prime number or the number 8?

5   Events A and B are mutually exclusive. If the probability that A occurs is $\frac{3}{8}$
   and the probability that B occurs is $\frac{1}{3}$, find the probability that:
   a) A or B occurs
   b) neither A nor B occurs
   c) A third event C occurs with a probability of $\frac{1}{2}$. Explain why the events A,
       B and C are not mutually exclusive.

38.3 and 38.4 Independent events and the multiplication principle

6 Which of the following pairs of events are independent?
   a) Two cards are picked from a pack of cards. The first card is replaced before the second is chosen.
   Event A: the first card is the Ace of hearts.
   Event B: the second card is a heart.
   b) Two cards are picked from a pack of cards. The first card is not replaced before the second is chosen.
   Event A: the first card is a diamond.
   Event B: the second card is the Queen of diamonds.
   c) Jenny and Joanne play a game of tennis.
   Event A: Jenny wins the first set.
   Event B: Jenny wins the second set.

7 The probability that Damien is selected for the school cricket team is $\frac{1}{10}$, for the school football team is $\frac{1}{15}$ and for both is $\frac{1}{40}$. Explain why being selected for the cricket team and being selected for the football team are *not* independent.

8 Mrs Jackson checks her car tyres every two weeks. Each tyre has a probability of 0.4 that it needs pumping up. What is the probability that all four tyres are below pressure?

9 Mrs Jackson also checks the oil level in the engine and the water in her windscreen washer. The probability that the oil needs topping up is 0.15 and the probability that the water needs topping up is 0.2. Find the probability that both need topping up next time she checks.

38.5 Tree diagrams

10 I shuffle a pack of cards and pick out a card at random. I look at it, and return it to the pack. I then shuffle the pack and pick out a card again. Copy and complete this tree diagram to represent the process.

First card	Second card	Outcome	Probability
	Ace	A,A	----------
Ace			
	not Ace	A,N	$\frac{1}{13} \times \frac{12}{13}$
	Ace	N,A	----------
not Ace			
	not Ace	N,N	----------

What is the probability that I have picked out at least one Ace?

11 Three babies are expected soon among the families living in my street. Copy and complete this tree diagram with three sets of branches. Use this to find the probability that there will be two girls amongst the three babies. Assume that the probability that a baby is a boy is $\frac{1}{2}$.

First baby	Second baby	Third baby		Outcome	Probability
			girl	G G G	- - - - - - - - - -
	girl		boy	G G B	- - - - - - - - - -
girl			girl	- - - - -	- - - - - - - - - -
	boy		boy	- - - - -	- - - - - - - - - -
			girl	- - - - -	- - - - - - - - - -
	girl		boy	- - - - -	- - - - - - - - - -
boy			girl	- - - - -	- - - - - - - - - -
	boy		boy	- - - - -	- - - - - - - - - -

12 The probability of tomorrow being fine is $\frac{3}{4}$. If it is fine, our football team has a probability of victory equal to $\frac{4}{5}$. If it is not fine, the probability of a win is only $\frac{1}{2}$.

Copy and complete this tree diagram to find the probability that the other team will win tomorrow's match.

Weather tomorrow	Outcome of match		Outcome	Probability
	$\frac{4}{5}$	win	fine, win	- - - - - - - - - -
	fine ?	lose	fine, lose	- - - - - - - - - -
$\frac{3}{4}$?		win	- - - - - - - -	- - - - - - - - - -
	wet ? ?	lose	- - - - - - - -	- - - - - - - - - -

13 Mr Williams has to pass through two sets of traffic lights on his way to work. The probability that he has to stop at the first set of lights is 0.5 and at the second set is 0.7.
Find the probability that he is held up at exactly one set of lights.

PROBLEM SOLVING

Journey graphs

Example

Jasmine and Caroline have a race over two lengths of a swimming pool. The distance-time graph for the race is shown below.

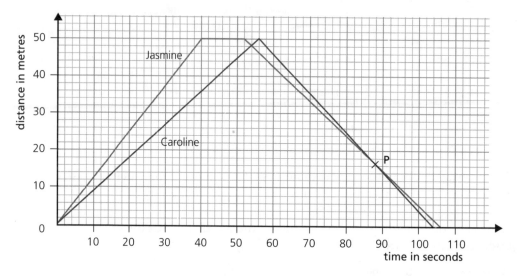

a) What is the length of the swimming pool?
b) Who swam faster at the start? How can you tell?
c) For what length of time are they swimming in opposite directions?
d) The graphs intersect at P. What happened at that time?
e) What was Jasmine's speed during the first length?
f) What was Caroline's average speed for the whole race?
g) Describe Jasmine's tactics.
h) Who won?

Answer
a) 50 m
b) Jasmine. Her graph is steeper than Caroline's at the start.
c) 4 seconds, i.e. between 52 and 56 seconds from the start.
d) Caroline overtook Jasmine.
e) 1.25 m/s. (This is given by the gradient of the line.)
f) 0.96 m/s. (Average speed = total distance ÷ total time.)
g) Jasmine swam the first length very fast and then rested at the far end. She set off again after 12 seconds, which allowed her to start the return journey ahead of Caroline.
h) Caroline.

Quadratic equations

Example

Solve these equations: a) $x^2 - 5x = 0$ b) $x^2 - 7x - 18 = 0$

Answer

a) Factorising gives $x(x - 5) = 0$, giving the solutions of the equation as $x = 0$ and $x = 5$.

b) Factorising gives $(x + 2)(x - 9) = 0$ i.e. $(x + 2) = 0$ or $(x - 9) = 0$. Hence the solutions are $x = -2$ and $x = 9$.

Writing the equation in this form we see that two numbers, namely x and $(x - 5)$, are multiplied together to make zero. This can only happen if either $x = 0$ or $x - 5 = 0$.

Further trial and improvement

The trial and improvement method is easier to work with if all the terms involving x are on one side of the equation. In some cases the equation may need to be rearranged first.

Example

One solution of the equation $\dfrac{1}{x} = 2x - 3$ is approximately 1.7.

Use trial and improvement to find this solution correct to 2 D.P.

Answer

$$\frac{1}{x} = 2x - 3 \qquad \text{\textit{Subtract }} \frac{1}{x} \text{ \textit{from both sides.}}$$

$$0 = 2x - \frac{1}{x} - 3 \qquad \text{\textit{Add 3 to both sides.}}$$

$$3 = 2x - \frac{1}{x} \qquad \text{i.e. } 2x - \frac{1}{x} = 3$$

We can now take $x = 1.7$ as a starting value and refine the solution by trial and improvement.

The solution is trapped between consecutive values to 2 D.P.

To decide on the best answer to 2 D.P. we must try the mid-value.

x	$2x - \dfrac{1}{x}$	
1.7	2.812	*too small*
1.8	3.044	*too large*
1.75	2.929	*too small*
1.78	2.998	*too small*
1.79	3.021	*too large*
1.785	3.010	*too large*

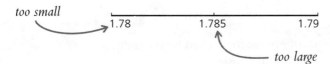

too small   1.78   1.785   1.79   *too large*

The required solution is 1.78 to 2 D.P.

Questions

39.1 Journey graphs

1   The diagram shows the progress of a train as a distance-time graph for the first 8 minutes of its journey after leaving a station.

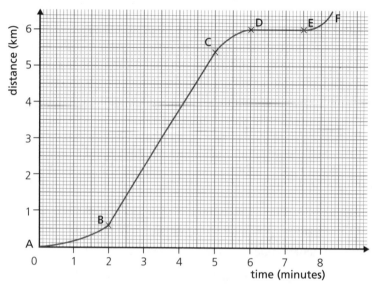

a) Describe what is happening in each of the stages AB, BC, CD, DE and EF.
b) How far does the train travel before its next stop?
c) Find the average speed of the train between stops in km/h.
d) What is the maximum speed of the train in km/h?

2   This is the speed-time graph of a train travelling between two stations.

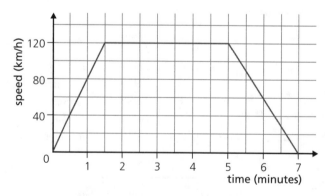

a) What is the maximum speed reached by the train?
b) How far apart are the stations?
c) What is the average speed of the train in km/h?

39.2 Quadratic equations

3 Solve these equations:
  a) $x(x - 9) = 0$ **b)** $x(x + 7) = 0$ **c)** $x^2 - 6x = 0$
  d) $x^2 - 8x + 5 = 5$ **e)** $(x - 6)(x + 7) = 0$ **f)** $(x - 6)^2 = 0$
  g) $x^2 + 3x = 7x$ **h)** $x^2 + 8x = 3x$ **i)** $x^2 + 4x - 8 = 7x - 8$

4 Copy and complete:
  a) $x^2 + 5x + 6 = (x + 3)(x + ...)$ **b)** $x^2 + 7x + 6 = (x + 1)(x + ...)$
  c) $x^2 + 9x + 20 = (x + ...)(x + ...)$ **d)** $x^2 + 11x + 24 = (x + ...)(x + ...)$
  e) $x^2 + 5x - 6 = (x + 6)(x ... ...)$ **f)** $x^2 + x - 20 = (x + ...)(x - ...)$
  g) $x^2 - 5x + 6 = (x - 3)(x - ...)$ **h)** $x^2 - 4x - 21 = (x + ...)(x - ...)$

5 Solve these quadratic equations by factorising first:
  a) $x^2 + 8x + 15 = 0$ **b)** $x^2 + 3x + 2 = 0$ **c)** $x^2 + 9x + 18 = 0$
  d) $x^2 + 3x - 18 = 0$ **e)** $x^2 - 11x + 30 = 0$ **f)** $x^2 - 10x + 25 = 0$

39.3 Further trial and improvement

6 The diagram shows the graphs of the equations
  $y = x^2$ and $y = 4x - 2$.

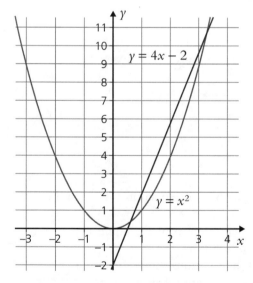

a) Explain how the diagrams show that the equation $x^2 - 4x = -2$ has two
  positive solutions.

b) Obtain initial estimates of these solutions from the diagram and use trial
  and improvement to refine them correct to 2 D.P.

7 The diagram shows
the graphs of
$y = \frac{5}{x}$ and
$y = 2x + 1$.

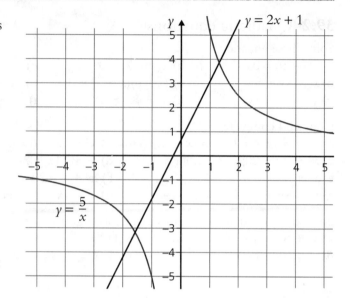

a) Use the diagram
to write down
initial estimates
of the solutions
to the equation
$\frac{5}{x} - 2x = 1$

b) Use trial and
improvement to
find both
solutions correct
to 2 D.P.

8 The diagram shows a sketch of the graph of the equation $y = 5 - x^2$.

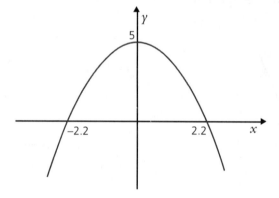

a) Copy the diagram and sketch the graph of the equation $y = \dfrac{1}{x}$ on the
same axes.

b) Find the equation satisfied by the x coordinates of any points common to
both graphs and state the number of solutions.

c) Estimate the approximate value of the solutions and use trial and
improvement to find the solutions correct to 2 D.P.

SINE, COSINE AND TANGENT

Providing we know the length of the hypotenuse and the other angles in a right-angled triangle, we can find the lengths of the other two sides.

The longest side is called the **hypotenuse**.

The side next to the known angle is called the **adjacent** side.

The side opposite the angle is called the **opposite** side.

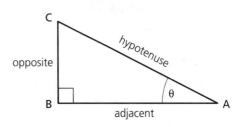

The length of any side can be found by choosing the appropriate expression from the following:

opposite = hypotenuse × sin θ	adjacent = hypotenuse × cos θ	opposite = adjacent × tan θ

These in turn can be re-arranged to give:

$$\sin\theta = \frac{\text{opposite}}{\text{hypotenuse}} \qquad \cos\theta = \frac{\text{adjacent}}{\text{hypotenuse}} \qquad \tan\theta = \frac{\text{opposite}}{\text{adjacent}}$$

The ratios sin θ, cos θ and tan θ are called **trigonometrical ratios** (or trig ratios). They are *only* true for right-angled triangles.

Example

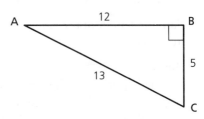

Write as a fraction:
a) sin A   b) cos A   c) tan C   d) cos C

Answer

For angle A: AC is the hypotenuse
                AB is the adjacent side
                BC is the opposite side.

For angle C: AC is the hypotenuse
                BC is the adjacent side
                AB is the opposite side.

a) $\sin A = \dfrac{\text{opposite}}{\text{hypotenuse}} = \dfrac{5}{13}$

b) $\cos A = \dfrac{\text{adjacent}}{\text{hypotenuse}} = \dfrac{12}{13}$

c) $\tan C = \dfrac{\text{opposite}}{\text{adjacent}} = \dfrac{12}{5}$

d) $\cos C = \dfrac{\text{adjacent}}{\text{hypotenuse}} = \dfrac{5}{13}$

Finding the length of a side

Providing we are given the length of one side (as well as the right angle) we can find the length of the other sides in the triangle. This is only true for right–angled triangles.

Example

Find the length of the side marked x (to 2 D.P.).

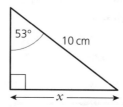

Answer

We know the hypotenuse is 10 cm.

The side x is *opposite* the angle we know, so we use the sin ratio.

opposite = hypotenuse $\times$ sin θ

We can now use this to find x.

$x = 10 \times \sin 53°$

$x = 7.99$ cm to 2 D.P.

Using a calculator key in: 10 ⊗ sin 53 =

or for some older calculators 10 ⊗ 53 sin =

Example

Find the length of the side marked x (to 1 D.P.).

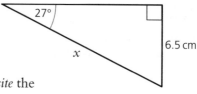

Answer

x is the hypotenuse. The 6.5 cm side is *opposite* the angle, so we need to use the sin ratio.

$\sin \theta = \dfrac{\text{opposite}}{\text{hypotenuse}}$ *Substitute in the formula.*

$\sin 27° = \dfrac{6.5}{x}$ *Multiply both sides by x.*

$x \times \sin 27° = 6.5$ *Divide both sides by sin 27°.*

$x = \dfrac{6.5}{\sin 27°} = 14.3$ cm (correct to 1 D.P.)

Using a calculator, key in: 6.5 ÷ sin 27 =

or for some older calculators 6.5 ÷ 27 sin =

Finding the size of an angle

Example

Find the size of angle θ (to 1 D.P.)

Answer

The side opposite the angle is 5 units.
The adjacent side is 12 units.

Using $\tan \theta = \dfrac{\text{opposite}}{\text{adjacent}}$

$\tan \theta = \dfrac{5}{12}$ giving $\theta = 22.6°$ to 1 D.P.

Using a calculator, key in: 5 12

or for some older calculators 5 12

Questions

40.1 and 40.2 Finding heights using sines and cosines

1   Find y in each of these right-angled triangles, using the sine formula:
opposite = hypotenuse $\times \sin \theta$.

a)

b)

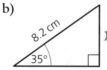

c)

d)

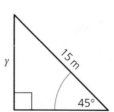

e)

2   Find x in each of these right-angled triangles, using the cosine formula:
    adjacent = hypotenuse × cos θ.

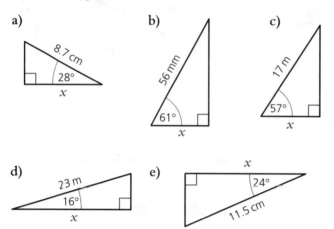

a)

b)

c)

d)

e)

40.3 to 40.5 Sines, cosines and tangents

3   Choose the appropriate trig ratio, sine, cosine or tangent, to find the length of
    the side marked d in each of these triangles.

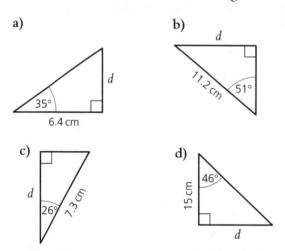

a)

b)

c)

d)

4   A woman 1.5 m tall observes that the angle of elevation to the top of a
    building 24 m away is 41°. What is the height of the building? Draw a sketch
    to help you.

5   One angle of a rhombus is 72°. The shorter diagonal is 8 cm long. Draw a
    sketch to help you.
    a) What are the sizes of the other angles?
    b) Find the length of the other diagonal.

6 a) For each triangle find the value of sin θ, cos θ and tan θ.

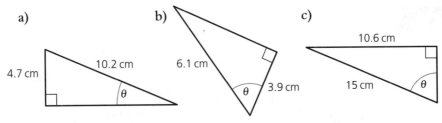

(i)   (ii)   (iii)   (iv)

b) What do you notice about your answers to (ii) and (iv)? Explain why this has happened.

7 Use your calculator to find the value of θ correct to 1 decimal place:
a) sin θ = 0.8763 b) sin θ = 0.2479 c) cos θ = 0.5861 d) tan θ = 0.8734

e) tan θ = 3.267 f) cos θ = $\frac{7}{16}$ g) sin θ = $\frac{15.3}{31.7}$ h) tan θ = $\frac{62.5}{11.9}$

i) tan θ = $\sqrt{3}$ j) cos θ = $\frac{\sqrt{3}}{2}$

8 Find θ in each of these triangles.

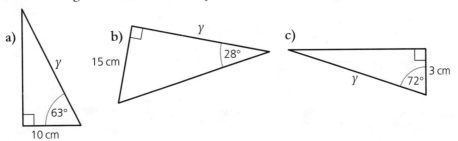

a)   b)   c)

9 A girl walks 1 km due East and then 2 km due South. Find her bearing from her original position. Draw a sketch to help you.

10 A pendulum swings so that the weight is 25 cm higher at the top of its swing than it is at the bottom. If the length of the string is 4 m, find the angle of swing on each side of the vertical. Draw a sketch to help you.

11 Find the length of the side marked y in each of these triangles.

a)
y
63°
10 cm

b)
15 cm
y
28°

c)
y
72°
3 cm

12   A walker on the top of a cliff 100 m high observes that the angle of depression to a boat at sea is 18°. How far is the boat from the cliff?

13   A plane flying at a height of 1000 metres is picked up on radar. How far is the plane from the radar if the angle of elevation is 27°?

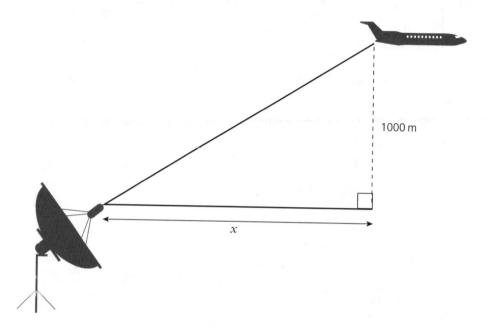

1000 m

x

EXAM PRACTICE

When working through the questions in this section, make a point of checking your answers as if you were in the examination. Ask yourself:

1   Have I answered the question?
2   Does the answer seem reasonable?

It's all too easy, under exam pressure, to misinterpret a question or to produce a silly answer. Carrying out these simple checks may help you spot the errors and save you valuable marks.

Number and algebra

1   The ratio of the volume of oil to the volume of vinegar in the French dressing used on salads is 5 to 2.
   a) How much oil must be added to 100 ml of vinegar to make some French dressing?
   b) A chef needs three and a half litres of French dressing for a big function. Calculate the volumes of oil and water needed.

2   A woman is x years old now. In 12 years time she will be three times as old as she was 12 years ago. Use this information to find the value of x.

3   Here is a number sequence: 2, 5, 10, 17, 26, ...
   a) Write down the seventh term.
   b) Write down the nth term.

4   a) Work through this number trick using algebra. It has already been started for you.

Think of a number	*Let the number be x*
Multiply it by five	*5x*
Add eight	
Subtract three	
Divide by five	
Subtract the number you first thought of	

   b) What do you notice about the final answer?

5   Farnham and Guildford lie on the road from Winchester to London. Farnham is one-third of the way and Guildford half the way. Take the distance from Winchester to London to be x miles. Express the distance between Farnham and Guildford in terms of x. If this is 10 miles, find the value of x.

6   150 people work in a small factory. One day 12 people were absent. What percentage of people were at work?

7   Here is part of a recipe for pancakes:

> ## Pancake mix
>
> *For 4 pancakes you will need:*
>
> 6 dessertspoons of flour
> $\frac{1}{2}$ pint milk
> 1 pinch of salt
> 1 egg

Jane wants to make 10 pancakes.
a) How much flour will she need?
b) How much milk will she need?

8   Solve this riddle by setting up and solving two simultaneous equations.
Tweedledum said to Tweedledee 'Your weight added to twice mine totals
361 pounds'. Said Tweedledee to Tweedledum 'Your weight added to twice
mine totals 362 pounds'.
How much did each weigh?

9   Over seventy million sets of the game Monopoly have been sold over the
years. Write this number in standard form.

10   Calculate **a)** $\dfrac{2}{\sqrt{5}-1}$ and **b)** the reciprocal of $\dfrac{2}{\sqrt{5}-1}$.
c) What do you notice about your two answers?

11   A forest fire spreads so that the number of hectares burnt after t hours
is given by:
$$h = 30(1.65^t)$$
According to this formula, what area would be burnt after 6 hours?

12   When $x + y = r$ and $x - y = s$:
a) Find $r + s$ in terms of x and y.
b) Find rs in terms of x and y.
c) When $x = 4$ and $y = -2$, find r.
d) When $r = 10$ and $s = -4$ find the values of x and y.

13   List the following in order of size, starting with the smallest:
0.8, $\frac{5}{7}$, 0.79, 9.8%

14   **a)** Simplify $4x^2 + 3x - x^2 + x$.
b) Factorise completely $12x - 8x^2$.
c) Expand and simplify $(x + 4)^2 - 3x$.

15 **a)** List the integer values of x that satisfy the condition $-5 < x - 1 \le 2$.

b) Solve the inequality $\dfrac{4x - 3}{2} > x + 1$.

16

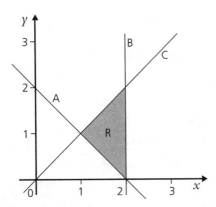

a) Write down the equations of the lines A, B and C.
b) Use three inequalities to describe the region R which includes the boundary lines.

17 **a)** *Estimate* the value of P given by:

$$P = \frac{19.7 \times 6.83}{11.8 + 1.95}$$

You *must* show all your working.
b) Use a calculator to find the value of P correct to three significant figures.
c) Explain why the following key sequence does not give the correct value of P.

19.7 $\boxed{\times}$ 6.83 $\boxed{\div}$ 11.8 $\boxed{+}$ 1.95 $\boxed{=}$

d) Write the expression that the sequence in part **c)** represents.

18 **a)** Find the reciprocal of (i) $\frac{3}{7}$ (ii) $1\frac{4}{7}$.

b) Calculate $11 \div 1\frac{4}{7}$. You *must* show your working.

19 Use trial and improvement to find a solution of the equation $x^2 + 5x = 8$ from a starting value of $x = 1.2$. Show all of your results and give the solution correct to two decimal places.

20 Use the formula $P = \sqrt{a^2 - 3b^2}$ to calculate the value of P, correct to two significant figures, given that $a = 8.73$ and $b = 1.29$.

21 **a)** Use the formula $v^2 = u^2 + 2as$ to find the value of v given that $u = -6.8$, $a = -1.2$ and $s = 5$.
b) Rearrange the formula to make s the subject.
c) Find the value of s when $v = 11.2$, $u = 0$ and $a = 9.8$.

Shape, space and measures

1

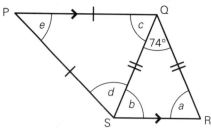

PQ = PS
QS = QR
PQ is parallel to SR.

a) Work out the sizes of the angles *a, b, c, d, e.*

b) Use your answers to **a)** to decide if PS is parallel to QR. Give reasons for your answer.

2 AB is a ladder leaning against a wall and touching an outbuilding at X.

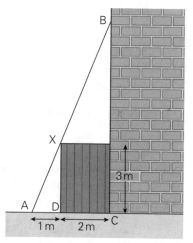

AD = 1 m, DC = 2 m, DX = 3 m.

a) Find the length of AX.

b) How far up the wall will the ladder reach?

c) How long is the ladder?

3 John designs an ornamental garden. There are four circular flower beds surrounded by gravel. There is a path around the outside. The diameter of each flower bed is 1 m.

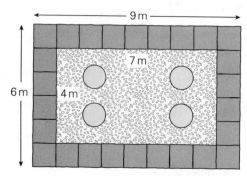

a) Calculate the area covered by gravel.

b) The gravel is spread to a depth of 5 cm. What volume of gravel is needed?

4

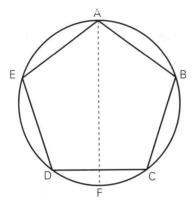

The shape ABCDE is a regular pentagon. AF is a diameter of the circle through the vertices of the pentagon.

a) Work out the size of angle CDE.

b) What is the size of angle ABF?

c) What is the size of angle DEF?

5 Rotherley, Donfield, Barncaster and Sheffham are four towns.

Donfield is 20 km from Rotherley on a bearing of 065°.

Sheffham is 8 km from Rotherley on a bearing of 225°.

Barncaster is 16 km from Rotherley on a bearing of 335°.

Using a scale of 1 cm to represent 2 km:

a) Draw a plan showing the positions of the towns.

b) What is the actual distance from Barncaster to Sheffham?

c) What is the bearing of Sheffham from Donfield?

6

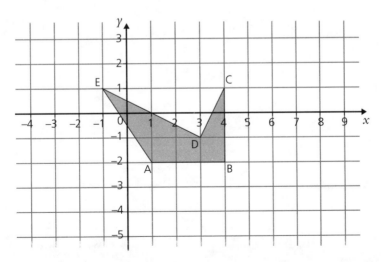

Using the origin as the centre of enlargement, enlarge the shape ABCDE by scale factor 2.

7 The diagram shows the plan of a field. A farmer wishes to put fencing around the sides A→B→C→D→A. The angle DAB is 50° and the side AB is 20 m long.

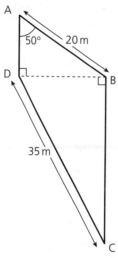

a) Work out the length of the side AD.

b) Side CD is 35 m long. Work out the length of side BC.

c) What is the size of angle BCD?

Handling data

1 This table shows the age distribution of females living in the UK.

Age	Number of females (millions)
0 to 9	3.7
10 to 19	3.4
20 to 29	4.4
30 to 39	4.0
40 to 49	3.9
50 to 59	3.0
60 to 69	2.9
70 to 79	2.4
80 to 89	1.5

Calculate an estimate of the mean age of females in the UK.

2 The table below shows the circulation in millions of some Sunday newspapers.
The third column shows the cost of a full page advert in each one.

Paper	Circulation (millions)	Cost of advert (thousands of pounds)
The Sunday Letter	2.0	28
News from the Planet	4.7	32
The Wayfinder	0.5	24
The Sunday Journal	2.6	29
Sunday News	3.5	30

a) Draw a scatter graph to represent this data.
b) Draw the line of best fit.
c) What would be a reasonable price for a full page advert in a Sunday
newspaper with a circulation of 1.2 million?

3   Old MacDonald keeps dairy cows. Half of them are Friesians and half are
    Jerseys. He records the amount of milk each group of cows produces each day
    for a month. Here are the results:

Milk yield (in litres)	Friesians	Jerseys
$140 \leq m < 145$	0	0
$145 \leq m < 150$	2	0
$150 \leq m < 155$	8	4
$155 \leq m < 160$	14	16
$160 \leq m < 165$	4	6
$165 \leq m < 170$	3	5
$170 \leq m < 175$	0	0

a) On the axes given, draw a frequency polygon for each group of cows.

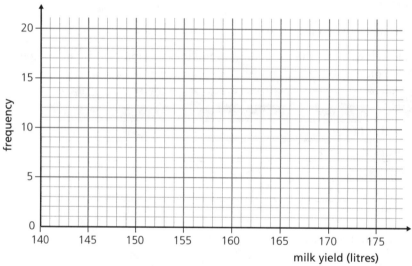

b) Which group of cows produced most milk?

4 The Year 7 Council at Willington School has eight members, Mark and Mandy from class 7M, Keith and Kate from class 7K, Harry and Helen from class 7H and Colin and Claire from class 7C.

They are to select two representatives for the School Council but they must not be both from the same class or the same sex.

a) Complete this list to show all the possible ways in which the representatives can be chosen. You will not need all the spaces.

Mark and Kate   ------------------   ------------------   ------------------

------------------   ------------------   ------------------   ------------------

------------------   ------------------   ------------------   ------------------

------------------   ------------------   ------------------   ------------------

b) What is the probability that Harry will be chosen?

c) Harry and Mandy are brother and sister and the headteacher will not allow two pupils from the same family on the School Council. What is the probability now that Harry will be chosen?

5 To win a car at the Summer Fayre, Colin has to throw 7 sixes with 7 dice. What is the probability that he will win the car with one throw of 7 dice?

6 This table gives the number of units of electricity used over a period of 200 days to heat the greenhouses at a garden centre.

Units of electricity	Frequency
1–10	1
11–20	6
21–30	18
31–40	25
41–50	38
51–60	45
61–70	32
71–80	22
81–90	10
91–100	3

a) Find the mean number of units of electricity used per day.

b) Draw up a cumulative frequency table and graph. Find the median number of units of electricity used.

7 The following table gives the frequency distribution of the examination marks of 900 students in an English examination.

Marks	Frequency
0–9	5
10–19	21
20–29	68
30–39	93
40–49	124
50–59	230
60–69	186
70–79	102
80–89	48
90–99	23

a) Calculate the mean.

b) Draw up a cumulative frequency table and graph. If the pass mark was set at 46 marks, how many candidates passed? An 'A star' grade was given to the top 10% of candidates. What was the lowest mark eligible for that grade?

8 A dice is thrown twice. Copy this tree diagram to help you answer the questions which follow.

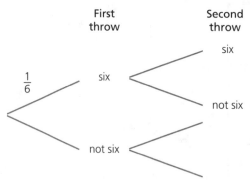

What is the probability of scoring:

a) two sixes

b) a six on either the first or the second throw

c) at least one six?

9 a) Four boys are picked at random from the whole school. What is the probability that they were all born on a Friday?

b) What is the probability that they were all born on the same day (any day of the week)?

CHECKLIST

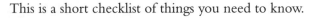

This is a short checklist of things you need to know.

1 Metric / Imperial equivalents

km to miles   litres to pints
cm to inches   litres to gallons
m to feet   kg to pounds

2 Formulae relating speed, distance and time

e.g. $\text{speed} = \dfrac{\text{distance}}{\text{time}}$

3 Graphs of equations
You should be able to recognise the graphs of equations that take these forms:

a) $y = mx + c$ (gradient $= m$, y-intercept $= c$)
b) $x + y = a$
c) $x = a,\ y = a$
d) $y = x^2$
e) $y = x^3$
f) $y = \dfrac{1}{x}$

4 Rules for simplifying expressions in algebra, and rules of priority when using a formula

5 Definitions when handling data
Discrete   Continuous
Mean   Median   Mode
Range   Interquartile range
Probability of equally likely outcomes
Relative frequency
Independent events   Mutually exclusive events
You need to know how to find the mean from a frequency table, and the median from a cumulative frequency graph.

6 Names and properties of various types of triangle and quadrilateral
Isosceles, equilateral
Square, rectangle, parallelogram, rhombus, kite, trapezium

7 Facts about angles including special results for parallel lines
Alternate angles, corresponding angles and vertically opposite angles

8 How to find the interior and exterior angles of polygons

9 Trigonometry
You need to know how to re-arrange the formulae given to you, e.g. that

$\text{opposite} = \text{hypotenuse} \times \sin\theta$ can be written as $\sin\theta = \dfrac{\text{opp}}{\text{hyp}}$.

FORMULAE SHEET

Area of triangle $= \frac{1}{2} \times$ base $\times$ height

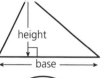

Circumference of circle $= \pi \times$ diameter
$= 2 \times \pi \times$ radius

Area of circle $= \pi \times (\text{radius})^2$

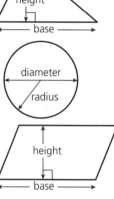

Area of parallelogram $=$ base $\times$ height

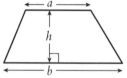

Area of trapezium $= \frac{1}{2}(a + b)h$

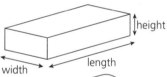

Volume of cuboid $=$ length $\times$ width $\times$ height

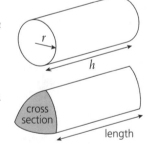

Volume of a cylinder $= \pi r^2 h$

Volume of a prism $=$ area of cross section $\times$ length

Pythagoras' theorem

$a^2 + b^2 = c^2$

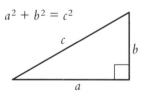

Trigonometry

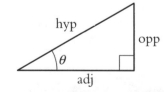

$\sin \theta = \dfrac{\text{opp}}{\text{hyp}}$

$\cos \theta = \dfrac{\text{adj}}{\text{hyp}}$

$\tan \theta = \dfrac{\text{opp}}{\text{adj}}$

or you could be given trig ratios as:
opposite $=$ hypotenuse $\times \sin \theta$
adjacent $=$ hypotenuse $\times \cos \theta$
opposite $=$ adjacent $\times \tan \theta$